Conflict and

By

W. H. R. RIVERS
M.D., D.Sc., LL.D., F.R.S.

CONTENTS

CONFLICT AND DREAM

CHAPTER I

FREUD'S THEORY OF DREAMS

DREAMS have always excited man's curiosity and
wonder, and there can be little doubt that they have
had a most important place in determining some of
the deepest and most widespread of his beliefs. In
the childhood of man one of his greatest difficulties
must have lain in his acquirement of the power to
distinguish the experience of the waking life from that
of sleep, and among many peoples, if not even sometimes among ourselves, the distinction is incomplete.
Not only have the occurrences of sleep had a large,
if not a preponderant, rôle in determining man's
belief in a spiritual world, but they must have taken
a large part in producing that mysterious aspect of its
experience which gives to religion in general its peculiar
character.

From quite early times it has been held that dreams
are not mere accidental occurrences of sleep, but have
a definite meaning. The interpretation of dreams
was very prominent in early literature, and in the
Old Testament it is assumed without question that
such dreams as those of Pharaoh and his servants
had definite meanings. Among nearly all peoples there
grew up definite systems of dream-interpretation,
according to which each image of a dream had a specific
meaning, and nearly all literatures, including our own,
have dream-books which give these meanings. Pharaoh
only became greatly exercised about his dreams of

the seven fat kine and the seven lean kine and of the seven full ears and the seven blasted ears of corn after his own wise men had failed to interpret them on the traditional lines of the time, so that a stranger had to be fetched out of prison to provide the solution.

In accordance with the spirit of that time the solution expected and given was of a prophetic kind. Dreams were regarded as means of foretelling the future, and this view is not only still widely held in popular belief, but it shows its influence also in the great importance attached to what is called the prospective value of the dream by one of the two chief schools of scientific dream-interpretation at the present time.

It is only during the last twenty years that we have made any real advance in the scientific study of the subject. Until still more recent times psychologists in general have paid but little attention to dreams.

When I suggested a question on dreams in a University examination not many years ago, it was objected that the students would know nothing about the subject, which meant, of course, that they had been taught nothing about it. The consideration of the psychology of dreams was not deemed worthy of inclusion in a course of academic psychology.

The great revolution in the attitude of psychologists which has since occurred is due to Freud—I think one might say entirely due to him. Among the many aspects of the vast influence which Freud has exerted upon psychology, none is more prominent than that concerned with dreams and their interpretation. It is natural, therefore, that I should make his work the starting-point of this discussion, and that a considerable part of the book will deal with criticism of his views.

I am very far from accepting everything that Freud has taught about the psychology of dreams, and I hope in this book to do my best to make clear where, in my opinion, his views should be accepted ; where

2

we must refuse to follow him ; and where our treatment, though running near his, should nevertheless diverge from it somewhat, either in its course or in its ultimate goal.

The first great contribution made by Freud to our understanding of the dream is his distinction between the manifest and the latent content. The older interpreters were chiefly interested in the incidents of the dream as actually experienced. If they dreamt of a death or a birth they were content if they were able to discover that on the previous day, or at some earlier time, they had seen a funeral or had heard of an addition to the family of an acquaintance. They gave no explanation of the irrational and fantastic character of the dream, nor did such explanation seem to them necessary. They were content to regard this character as proper to the dream and as no more in need of explanation than the imaginative character of poetry or the mournful nature of a tragedy. Even now there are prominent " scientific " writers who believe that they have provided a sufficient explanation of a dream when they have been able to refer its incidents to associations arising out of waking experience.

By Freud the features of the dream as experienced and related by the dreamer are spoken of as the manifest content, and this is only regarded as of interest in that it is held to be the expression of a deeper meaning, an expression of thoughts which Freud calls the latent content. This distinction between the manifest and latent contents and the view that the manifest content is an expression of a deeper meaning, are the most important and essential features of Freud's scheme of dream-interpretation.

A second feature is that, according to Freud, this deeper meaning always takes the form of the fulfilment of a wish, and that, the manifest content of the dream is the expression in more or less symbolic form of some

3

desire of the dreamer. I may say here at once that while I accept without hesitation Freud's distinction between the manifest and latent contents of the dream, I regard the view that every dream is a wish-fulfilment as an inadequate expression of the relation between the two kinds of content. A large part of this book will be devoted to a criticism of this aspect of Freud's position, and an endeavour to state a different point of view.

A third feature of Freud's scheme is that the manifest content becomes the expression of the wish through a process of distortion, whereby the real meaning of the dream is disguised from the dreamer. Freud believes that it is the function, or one of the functions, of the dream to protect the sleeper from thoughts which might so disturb him if they reached his consciousness that he would awake. The dream is regarded as the guardian of sleep. Freud believes that in the dream the disturbing thoughts are so distorted and disguised that their real nature is not recognised by the sleeping-consciousness. This again is a subject in which I shall not be able to follow Freud faithfully. Consequently I shall not speak of the process by which the manifest content is produced as a distortion of the latent content, but shall use the word " transformation " in its place. I shall speak of the manifest content of the dream as coming into being by a process of transformation of a wish or other form of latent content.

I propose to leave until the next chapter an account of the processes by which this transformation is effected, the processes which Freud has summed up under the general title of the " dream-work." I shall only mention now one other feature of his scheme of dream-interpretation. According to Freud the process of transformation, or, as he would call it, distortion, is due to the necessity of overcoming resistance to the appearance of the latent content in consciousness,

4

even in the form of a dream. It is supposed that the manifest dream is an occurrence in which experience appears in the consciousness of sleep which has been banished from the consciousness of the waking life by processes of repression or suppression, and that the process of transformation is necessary in order to overcome a resistance to his appearance. Freud has given a metaphorical expression to this resistance by the use of the simile of the social process of censorship. He supposes that the experience kept out of the consciousness of waking life can only find access to the consciousness of sleep if it suffers such transformation or distortion that its real meaning will not be recognised by the sleeper. The feature of resistance thus presented to the direct and undisguised appearance of the latent content Freud calls censorship.

I must be content with this general sketch of Freud's scheme of dream-interpretation. I propose now to give a brief account of the history of my own attitude towards the scheme; one which I believe to represent that of many students of the older psychology.

Though I had taken much interest in the general views of Freud before the war, I had not attempted to master his theory of dreams. I was more interested in the applications of his scheme to the explanation of psychoneurosis and the anomalous behaviour of everyday life. When the war brought me into touch with dreams as prominent symptoms of nervous disorder and as the means of learning the real nature of the mental states underlying the psychoneuroses of war, it became necessary to study Freud's scheme of dream-interpretation more closely, and I read his book carefully. This reading, however, left a most unsatisfactory impression on my mind. The interpretations seemed to me forced and arbitrary, and the general method of so unscientific a kind that it might be used to prove anything. Let me give one or two instances.

5

FREUD'S THEORY OF DREAMS

Freud claims that several of his patients' dreams depended upon the desire to convict Freud himself of error when he assumed the nature of dreams to be wish-fulfilments, and yet he continues, apparently without hesitation, to rely upon the analysis of his own dreams, in which the desire to show the rightness of his views must have been a far stronger motive than, or at least as strong a motive as, could have been present in the case of his patients.

Again, the idea that an event of a dream may indicate either one thing or its opposite, gives an arbitrary character to the whole process of dream-interpretation, which must be most unsatisfactory to anyone accustomed to scientific method. One of Freud's rules of interpretation is that every element of the dream may be interpreted by its opposite as well as by itself, and that only the connections of the dream can enable the interpreter to decide in favour of one or the other. Such a method would reduce any other science to an absurdity, and doubts must be raised whether psychology can have methods of its own which would make it necessary to separate it from all other sciences and put it in a distinct category. At this time I had little opportunity for testing dream-interpretation practically. I was serving in a hospital for private soldiers, where the idea had got about that dreams were used by the medical officers as means of testing whether their patients were to be sent back to France, and it was only rarely that one was able to obtain more than the merest fragments of a dream. Such dreams as were related by my patients were usually of a very simple kind and, so far as they went, furnished confirmation of Freud's view that dreams have the fulfilment of a wish as their motive.* Thus, one soldier

---

* In this paragraph I think Dr Rivers underestimates the extent of the experience of dream-interpretation he acquired at the Maghull Hospital, and especially the part such experience played in shaping his own views on the rôle of conflict.—G. E. S.

6

dreamt that he was sent back to the front, but directly he landed in France, peace was declared.

In October 1916 I was transferred to a hospital for officers, where I soon began to obtain from my patients dreams of a less simple kind, but I made no great progress in dream-analysis or in the clinical utilisation of dreams until I had a dream myself which went far to convince me of the truth of the main lines of the Freudian position. Before I record this dream I should like to say a few words about my method of dream-interpretation, which differs in some important respects from that of most other workers, especially those of the psycho-analytic school. In the interpretation of dreams by the dreamer himself, it is customary to use the method adopted in the psycho-analytic investigation of others, and to make each image or incident of the dream the starting-point of a process of free association. It is believed by Freud and his followers that the thoughts coming into the mind in association with the image or incident of the dream will lead back to the dream thought which formed the corresponding feature of the latent content.

As I have said, my own method is different. In order to make its nature clear, I must describe a special feature of my mental make-up which I have utilised in this process.

For many years I have been the habitual subject of an experience in which, as soon as I become aware that I am awake, I find that I am thinking, and have for some time been thinking, over some problem, usually in connection with the scientific work upon which I am at the time engaged. Many of the scientific ideas which I value most, as well as the language in which they are expressed, have come to me in this half-sleeping, half-waking state directly continuous with definite sleep. When I began to analyse my dreams I frequently had a similar experience in which as soon as I was awake I found that I was already having, and had for some time been having, thoughts about a dream, the dream itself being still clearly in my mind. In some cases it was difficult to say where the dream ended and the unwitting analysis had begun, but a distinction was usually possible, owing to my lack of imagery when awake.* I could be confident that so long as the experience was accompanied by definite imagery, it was that of a dream or of a dream-like state, while the period when imagery was absent was one in which I was no longer dreaming, though I may not yet have realised that I was awake.

This peculiarity of my experience of the process of awaking introduces a special feature into the records and analyses of my own dreams. There can be little question that the ideal condition for an irreproachable analysis of a dream is one in which the dream is fully recorded before the analysis begins. In this case all danger is avoided that elements derived from, or suggested by, the analysis may be incorporated into the tissue of the dream. In many cases in which I awoke from a dream more or less suddenly I was able to fulfil this ideal condition, but in the frequent cases in which the dream passed insensibly into the half-waking, half-sleeping and unwitting process of analysis, the danger to which I have referred cannot be excluded. The comparison of dreams so analysed, or partially so analysed, with those where the act of awaking was sudden shows, however, that there is little or no difference between them, and I am inclined to regard my unwitting or partially unwitting method of analysis as one especially likely to lead one to the real thoughts and emotions forming the latent content of the dream.

In other cases, after having fully awaked and re-

---

* See *Instinct and the Unconscious*, Cambridge, 1920; 2nd Edition, 1922. The page references given elsewhere in this book apply equally to both editions.

corded the dream, I would fall into the half-waking, half-sleeping state, and not infrequently it was in this state that the thoughts came which furnished the explanation of the dream. In more than one case this later period of sleepiness passed into one which must be regarded as sleep, for the clue to the nature of the dream came as a definite image. In this case we may regard the interpretation of a dream as having been furnished by a second dream, even though, as a matter of fact, this second dream may have consisted only of a single image.

Where the solution of the dream failed to come in this more or less spontaneous way, I adopted the more usual procedure of turning my attention to different elements of the manifest content, allowing any associations so aroused to pass through my mind. I also searched the experience of the day or two before the dream which could have taken part in determining the nature of the manifest content, and in some cases found that the experience which had determined the manifest content was of distinct service in the process of reaching the deeper meaning of the dream. When I had reached what seemed to me to be the interpretation of the dream, I wrote out the analysis as fully as possible and, except in a few cases, the exceptions being definitely noted in my records, the complete analysis of the dream had been made and recorded before breakfast on the morning immediately following the dream.*

THE " PRESIDENCY " DREAM

I can now return to my dream. I dreamt I was in a Cambridge College garden—not the garden of any one college, but it was thought of vaguely, in the manner

* Other aspects of this problem are discussed in Chapter IV on Methods of Dream-Analysis.

so characteristic of the dream, as a kind of composite of the gardens of three colleges of which Pembroke was perhaps the most prominent. In this dream-garden I met my friend Professor X, with whom I entered into conversation   I did not remember what we said, but when I left him I went towards a building with the idea that a meeting of the Council was being held there, and, more vaguely, that the Council in question was that of the Royal Anthropological Institute of which both Professor X and I were members. As I was entering the room I hesitated, because it occurred to me that they might be discussing some matter in which I was myself concerned. I entered, however, and found a number of people sitting round a table whom, with one exception, I did not know. The exception was a prominent member of the Council of the Institute who was reading a list of names, which I took to be those of the persons who were being proposed as members of the Council for the ensuing year. I failed to recognise these names as those of any persons I knew.* When the reader had finished, he put the paper from which he had been reading on the table, and I leaned over to look at it, in order to ascertain who had been nominated as President, for I knew that his name would appear at the head of the list of new members of Council   There I read

S. Poole.

In the thoughts which followed, when from later experience I can be fairly certain that I was in the half-

---

* The fact that the persons proposed for membership of the Council were all unknown to me has some interest.   It has often been in my thoughts how large a proportion of members of the Council are unknown as anthropologists, and it is more than probable that my failure to recognise the names of the persons proposed at the dream-meeting is connected with this opinion.   It is noteworthy that the " prominent member of the Council " who read the list is a representative of the older school of anthropologists whose influence is sometimes a matter of annoyance to me in connection with the management of the affairs of the Institute.

waking state, I thought of the name as connected with Stanley Pool, the great bend of the Congo, while the person who came into my mind was Professor Lane-Poole, the Orientalist. I wondered why, if they were choosing an Oxford scholar, they had not rather chosen Professor Haverfield, whose work seemed to me to lie nearer the interests of the Institute. About this stage I became aware of the fact that I was in bed and that the experience through which I had just passed was that of a dream. Interested as I was at the time in dream-interpretation, it was natural that I should begin a process of analysis, or rather continue the analysis which had already begun in the thoughts of the half-waking state which I have already related. The first fact which occurred to me was that it was about the date at which the meeting would normally occur at which the President and Council of the Institute for the ensuing year would be chosen. I was also aware that my name would almost certainly have been considered for the position of President if I had not been working at so great a distance from London. Some time earlier I had discussed the question whether I should accept the Presidency, if it were offered to me, with Professor X who had appeared in the dream. In this conversation I had made clear a definite conflict which was present in my mind in relation to the position. On the one side was a natural desire to hold a position of honour, the leading position in connection with anthropology in Great Britain, and one which, for certain family reasons,* I should especially value. The motives on the other side were that its duties would involve a great deal of time and trouble ; that the business of presiding at meetings was highly irksome to

---

* This reason was that my mother's brother, James Hunt, had been one of the founders and the first President of the Anthropological Society of London, one of the two societies by the fusion of which the Institute was formed.

me, and that I had certain disqualifications for the post, especially the stammering to which I am liable when I have to make speeches of a ceremonial kind, such as inevitably fall to the lot of a President. I had gone over these reasons in my conversation with Professor X, and had then inclined to the view that I would, on the whole, prefer not to hold the position, rather with the idea that, as a result of our conversation, it might not be offered to me, for I suspected that I should not have the strength of mind to refuse it if it were actually offered.

It will thus be obvious that there were amply sufficient grounds for a conflict of a definite kind. Though I was not aware that the matter had been active in my thoughts at the time, I knew that the Presidency for the ensuing year would be decided about this time, and the receipt of the journal *Man*,* which would have reached me a day or two earlier, might well have tended to arouse the conflict.

A meeting of the Council of the Anthropological Institute being thus natural as the subject-matter of a dream, it remained to discover why the dream should have taken its especial form, and why the name " S. Poole " should have appeared in place of my own name, if the dream were the fulfilment of a wish that I should be nominated as President. It soon became obvious— I was not aware of any difficulty in reaching the conclusion—that the name I saw on the paper of the dream was a transformation of my own name, and my first impression was that the initial " S " was the final letter of my own surname transposed so as to become the initial of a baptismal name. As is every boy whose name is derived from a natural object, I had been miscalled Streams, Waters, and other variants at school,

* On the cover of this journal it is customary to print a list of the names of the office-bearers and Council of the Royal Anthropological Institute.

but so far as I could recollect, my name had never in actual life taken the form assumed in the dream, but I had no doubt that the dream-name was only another such variant.* The dream thus seemed to furnish confirmation of two of the most important features of Freud's scheme : his theory of the dream as a wish-fulfilment and his view that the manifest content is a transformation of this latent wish of such a kind that is not recognised by the sleeper, but only becomes apparent through a process of interpretation in the waking state, and in the vast majority of dreams never becomes apparent at all. In this case the transformation was even of a kind to which the term distortion might legitimately be applied.

The use of a certain disposition of water in Nature in place of that to which my proper name has reference might also be regarded as an example of that mechanism of the dream-work which Freud calls displacement. The interest attendant upon seeing my own name in a certain connection had been transferred from that name to one which had no significance for me while dreaming and only became significant through a process of examination after waking.

My impression at the time, then, was that two prominent features of Freud's scheme of dream-formation found striking confirmation in the example I have related. Before I consider the matter critically, however, it may be well to examine certain features of the manifest dream more closely with the aim of discovering how they were determined. It is necessary to explain why the name " S. Poole " should have taken the place of my own ; why the letter " e " should have appeared at the end of the word " pool," which would be the more natural variant of my name ; why the final letter of my own name should either have

* For another example of a pun on the name Rivers, see the Transference Dream in Chapter II, page 32.

disappeared or have been transferred to the beginning ; and why Professor Lane-Poole and Stanley Pool should have been so prominent in the thoughts of the half-waking state which immediately followed the dream.

As I have already said, my first impression was that the " S " of the dream-name was the transposed final letter of my own name, a transposition which would be assisted by my familiarity as an anthropologist with Stanley Pool as a geographical expression. The first step in the further analysis of these features of the manifest content occurred at breakfast on a morning following the dream. On relating the dream to my colleagues one of them told me that Dr Lane-Poole's Christian name was Stanley, a fact of which I was certainly not manifestly aware. It became evident that if I could discover why Dr Lane-Poole's name had taken the place of my own, I should also obtain the explanation of the prominence of " Stanley Pool " in the thoughts following the dream.

The next step in the analysis of the manifest content occurred a day or two later when glancing through the *Scotsman* I found the name of Lieutenant S. Pool among those who had received the Military Cross. As Lieutenant Pool was a member of the R.A.M.C., it occurred to me that I might have seen his name before my dream in one of the medical papers, and on consulting the *British Medical Journal* of 2nd December, I found not only that the name was there in the form " Temp. Lieut. Samuel Pool, M.B., R.A.M.C.," but that it occupied a prominent position at the head of a column,* so that it would almost certainly have struck the eye of anyone reading through the list. I had no doubt that I had seen the paper, as it was my habitual practice to read it, but I had no witting memory of having done so, or of having seen the name in

* *Brit. Med. Jour.*, 2nd December 1916, page 775.

14

question. If, as I have no doubt, I had seen this name, it would have helped to determine the special form assumed by the dream-surrogate of my name. If the initial S was the transposed end-letter of my name, it would have helped to determine this transposition.

A more difficult topic was the substitution of Dr Lane-Poole for myself, and on this I could for some time obtain no light whatever. Several weeks later, however, a patient who was leaving the hospital returned to me a book-catalogue which I had lent him. The patient was a theological student and the catalogue was one of theological and Oriental books, and, on looking through it, I found that Dr Lane-Poole's name occurred in it in the form " S. Lane-Poole." I do not know when I looked through this catalogue, or even with certainty whether I had read it at all, though it is very unlikely that I omitted to do so before lending it. I tried to discover from the bookseller exactly when it was sent to me, but without success, and I must be content to mention the possibility that this catalogue may have furnished the occasion for the appearance of Dr Lane-Poole in my dream-thoughts, and consequently for the final letter of my dream-name.

Of the various elements of the process by which my name was transformed in the dream, that which will arouse most doubt—it certainly gave me such doubts— is the transposition by which the final letter of my own name became an initial letter of my dream-name. It is therefore of interest that, through the kindness of Mrs Eder, I am able to give a similar example of this process. One of her patients had a dream in which he saw the following name :

L. Pestiles.

Associations with this word gave both " pastilles " and " Bastille," both of which words contain a double

15

l in place of the single *l* of the dream-name. It is highly probable that here also we have to do with a case of transposition of a letter, in this case a transposition from its proper position in the middle of two words to become the initial letter of a dream-name.

Having now explained as far as possible how the manifest content of the dream was determined, I can return to consider more closely how far the dream is in harmony with Freud's scheme. There is no question concerning one most important feature of this scheme. In the dream an outstanding, indeed the essential, element of the latent content appeared in such a guise that its nature was not recognised by myself so long as I was asleep. A wish that I should be chosen to be president of a society was disguised by the appearance of my name in a distorted form. The dream differed from many of the dreams of adults, or at any rate of educated adults, in that in other respects the manifest content of the dream was closely connected with the wish that formed its motive. Though there was the fantastic feature that a meeting of the Council of a London Society took place in an outhouse of a Cambridge College garden, a feature that is possibly connected with my objection to the journeys to London which the Presidency would involve, the actual setting of the dream was just such a meeting of the Council of the Society as would normally decide the choice of a new President, and the chief actors were not disguised, but their identity was clearly recognised in the dream, being people active in the affairs of the Society. Indeed, it was the unusually small amount of transformation or distortion in the dream as a whole which made it so easy to recognise the transformation which produced its culminating feature. It was the small amount of transformation, or rather its limitation to the central point of the dream, which made the process so obvious.

I have so far assumed that the dream I have related provides a good example of the fulfilment of a wish, and I may now consider this matter more fully. When looked at from one point of view, the appearance of my name, though in transformed character, as President of a Society was undoubtedly the fulfilment of a wish which was clearly present in my mind, at any rate beneath the surface, but this wish was in conflict with other wishes. To say that the dream I have related expressed the fulfilment of a wish seems too simple a way of expressing the situation. The dream was rather the expression of a conflict between a number of wishes, or more accurately between a number of conative trends, some of which might be called wishes, while others were rather of the nature of fears or apprehensions. I prefer, therefore, to regard the dream as the expression of a conflict, and as an attempt to solve the conflict by such means as are available during sleep.

If we regard mental experience as being arranged in strata or levels comparable with those which we now believe to be represented in the nervous system, the dream may be regarded as the solution of a conflict by means of processes belonging to those levels of activity which are still active in sleep. In setting-out, therefore, on our study of dream-psychology in this book, I propose to regard Freud's formula as unduly simple, and suggest as an alternative the working hypothesis that the dream is the solution or attempted solution of a conflict which finds expression in ways characteristic of different levels of early experience.* It will become our business to inquire not only whether this hypothesis is capable of explaining the many

---

* For a preliminary statement of this position, see my paper on " Freud's Concept of the Censorship " in *The Psycho-analytic Review*, republished as one of the Appendices in *Instinct and the Unconscious*. The view now put forward is formulated especially on pages 230-232 of the latter work.

varieties of the experience of sleep, but also whether the adoption of modes of expression characteristic of different periods of life bears any relation to the character of the desire or other state which is finding expression in the dream.

CHAPTER II

THE DREAM-WORK

In the first chapter I dealt especially with those parts of
Freud's scheme of dream-interpretation according to
which the manifest dream, the dream as we experience
it, is the fulfilment of a latent desire in the dreamer's
mind, expressing itself in a symbolic form through the
intermediation of a process of transformation or, as
Freud prefers to call it, distortion.

I left on one side the nature of this process of transformation or distortion, a process which Freud has
called "the dream-work." I propose now to begin
the consideration of the processes which make up this
dream-work.

Freud himself distinguishes four main processes :
(i) condensation ; (ii) displacement ; (iii) plastic representation, and (iv) secondary elaboration.

The first of these, condensation, is a process with
which it is not necessary to deal at length because,
in my opinion, it is not a process which is especially
characteristic of the dream, but is a feature of every
mental process, waking or sleeping It is just as much
a character of mental products in general as of the
dream. If you take any of the ideas which I am now
trying to bring before you, or any of the images which
may be called up in your minds on hearing my words,
you will find that there is condensed in each of them
a vast mass of experience derived both from the conversation and reading of everyday life and from special
studies. In exactly the same way it is possible to

show that any image or incident of a dream is the product of a process of condensation in which many different experiences have converged. Thus, to take an example from the dream considered in Chapter I, the dream-name " S. Poole " was found to have been determined, partly by a fanciful resemblance to my own name ; partly by the fact that a similar name had been seen in a medical paper a day or two earlier ; partly perhaps by the fact that I had noticed the name of Dr Lane-Poole in a book-catalogue, and partly by my anthropological interests which would have given to some chance reference to Stanley Pool more meaning to me than it would have had to another person. Moreover, it is probable that a deeper analysis than that carried out by myself would have led to other elements of experience which had taken a part in determining that S. Poole should have been nominated by the dream-consciousness as a substitute for myself.

The second process singled out by Freud is that he calls displacement (Verschiebung). I believe that this process, as described by Freud, is one in which several processes are combined which should properly be distinguished from one another. I shall only mention here one to which Freud ascribes especial importance, according to which the image or incident which is most important in the manifest dream is not a symbol of the most important latent dream-thought, but is an image of an indifferent kind to which the interest of the latent thought has been displaced. If again I take my " Presidency " dream as an example, it cannot be regarded as an example of a displacement of this kind. There can be little question that the prominent image of the dream was the name of S. Poole of the dream-president, and few, I think, will question that the prominent feature of the latent dream-thoughts was my repressed wish to be President.

There was displacement in that the interest in myself as President was transferred to the neutral personage S. Poole, of the dream, but there was no displacement of the kind which Freud regards as the most characteristic form of the process.

The third element which Freud finds in the dream-work, that which he calls plastic representation, is one the nature of which can be made clearer if we distinguish in it two different processes, symbolisation and dramatisation. By means of the first of these two processes the latent dream-thoughts find expression by means of symbols. The images of a dream are symbols of the elements which enter into the conflict by which, as was explained in the last chapter, the dream has been determined. The process of dramatisation is closely connected with this use of symbols. The dreamer sees in the dream persons moving before him and events happening which give it a dramatic character by which the conflict is made concrete and, though in altered guise, conspicuous.

The dream related in Chapter I is not a good example of either of these processes. The Presidency dream had a certain dramatic character, but this was of much the same nature as that of the process, viz., the choice of a President, which the dream was illustrating, and the S. Poole of the dream can hardly be regarded as a good example of a symbol. I propose to devote the larger part of this chapter to the consideration of a dream which illustrates far more aptly these two processes of symbolisation and dramatisation.

I do not propose to speak at length about Freud's fourth process of the dream-work, that which he calls secondary elaboration. This is a process in which the dream as experienced is modified and altered in the process of relating it or of recalling it if it has disappeared, or seems to have disappeared, from memory. As will be evident, it is a process of great importance whenever we are trying to estimate the value of a dream as evidence, whether for some practical purpose, such as medical diagnosis, or for some scientific purpose, such as that of discovering the nature of the mental processes by which the character of dreams in general is determined, but it is not in itself a process of any great scientific interest, and I shall say little about it in this book.

I can now turn to the dream by means of which I propose to illustrate these processes of the dream-work. It is a dream of one of my patients, a medical man with the rank of captain in the R.A.M.C. who had served in France. This service, and especially certain experiences centring round the death of a French prisoner who had been mortally wounded during his escape from the German lines, had given him such a horror of medical practice that he was extremely reluctant to return to the practice of his profession. His relatives, and especially his wife's people who came from Canada, unaware of the real motives of this reluctance, were using all their influence to induce him to return to medical practice. Shortly before the dream he had talked over the whole situation with me, and I had suggested that he should take up " Public Health," where he would rarely, if ever, be subjected to experiences which would recall the horrors of his war service. A few days later he sent me an account of the dream by which I propose to illustrate the nature of the processes of symbolisation and dramatisation.

THE " SUICIDE " DREAM

I give this dream in the form in which it was recorded for me by my patient, whom I will call " Captain."

" I was seated in the front of the stalls at the Golders Green Empire. I was to give a speech on ' The Present

22

Struggle.' I felt extremely nervous, because I was of two minds on the subject on which I had to speak. You were on the stage with me when I mounted it, and everybody I knew and had known seemed to be there. Gathering courage I commenced: 'Ladies and Gentlemen, I desire to address you on "The Present Struggle."' Even as I started speaking I noticed that the seat I had just left was occupied by a man, though I had not seen him come in. I felt compelled to address myself to this man in particular. He appeared to be a stranger to me, yet there was something familiar about him. He looked like a Viking, that is, so far as his complexion, hair and eyes were concerned. I mean that his eyes shone fiercely blue and his hair seemed luminous gold.

" I resumed: 'We must continue the struggle to the last man. Better let us die than lose our manhood and independence and become the slaves of an alien people.'

" The man in the seat seemed to become intensely depressed as I said these words. Yet, though he approved, my words seemed to arouse some dissent in other parts of the hall, and it was then that I noticed that there were two stewards, one at each exit. The steward on my left was a Canadian with the face of my father-in-law, and the man on my right was Dr X, wearing his post-mortem apron and gloves. I continued pointing out how everything depended upon our putting out our mightiest fight. The man in my chair cheered and his eyes shone.

"'Silence there,' threatened the Canadian, 'or I'll deal with you,' as he glanced at the man in my chair. 'I'll give you a taste of this,' and he held up a stick towards the man. Then I noticed that a snake was crawling up the stick and it seemed to menace the man in my seat. I was filled with horror, and then I noticed that the man in my chair had changed. As he looked

23

at the Canadian his eyes became dark and filled with
infinite suffering and he seemed to be almost another
person, for his hair had become dark and his skin was no
longer fair. He so affected me that I became less
confident. ' I know,' I said, ' that we have suffered
and are all suffering dreadful agony.' At this the man
in my chair, still dark in eye and face, groaned aloud
in agony.

" ' What rest peace would bring us all,' I continued.
The man's eyes now showed such agony that I felt it
would be merciful if I killed him immediately, and
Dr X seemed to read my thoughts, for he smiled.
' I'll deal with him,' shouted the Canadian, and putting
his stick with the snake down, he held up a lady's
corset and cried : ' I've a straight-waistcoat for him.'
Here you interposed from the platform saying, ' Order
there. Let the man alone. Go on, Captain. The
fellow is ill, very ill.'

" Taking courage I went on, telling them that despite
our intense suffering we must go on. ' There must
be no surrender. We must not give in.' Again the
man in my seat became a different being. His stature
seemed to increase. Again his eyes seemed to shine
blue fire, his hair was of gold and he cheered aloud.
This enraged the Canadian at the exit and he again
lifted the stick with the snake writhing on it. ' I'll
give him a taste of this,' he shouted, and the man in
my chair seemed to shrink. Again he was suffering
dreadfully and I could not bear to see it. His eyes
showed such agony that I felt I must kill him. Dr
X smiled grimly and approvingly at me and shouted :
' This way for the Angel of Peace.' You then interposed, saying that the man was so ill. I said : ' I'll
put him out of his misery,' and took up a revolver
which lay on the table. ' He won't feel it,' I said,
' there will be no blood and he will stop breathing at
once.' ' Don't do it,' you said, ' the man is ill, but he

will get well.' I could no longer stand the look in
the man's eyes and determined to shoot. I was just
raising the revolver when I heard the voice of my son
saying, ' Don't do it, daddy, you'll hurt me too.'
" I woke, feeling ill and very depressed. It seemed
very terrible and was the worst dream I ever had in
my life."

I knew the patient so well that I was able to interpret
nearly every feature of the dream at once. From
boyhood the patient had wished that he had been fair
and had had blue eyes, and this wish, combined with
the fact that the man occupied his seat in the audience
left no doubt whatever in my mind that the man in
the patient's chair was the dream-substitute of the
patient himself. We can with confidence interpret
the dream-experiences of the man in the audience
as those of the patient. I recognised at once that the
Canadian who had the face of his father-in-law represented his wife's people, and that the stick with the
snake first creeping up it and then writhing round
it was a symbol of Medicine, with which his wife's
people were, in fact, threatening him. Dr X, the
guardian of one of the exits of the hall, was a friend
of the dreamer who had recently committed suicide,
whence his approval of the resolve of the patient to
shoot the man in the audience. As this man was the
dream-surrogate of the patient, the shooting, if it
had taken place, would have been a dream-homicide
symbolising an act of suicide, the suicidal nature of
the act being disguised by the transformation of the
dream in which the patient was represented by the man
in the audience.

The voice of the sleeper's child in the dream represented the element in the conflict arising out of the
social sentiment whereby a suicide inflicts a stigma
upon those he leaves behind him.

The attitude towards the corset waved before the man in the audience undoubtedly represents the relation of the dreamer towards his wife, but the record of the dream leaves the exact nature of this relation doubtful. The eyes of the man again became blue and his skin fair after the incident of the corset, but it is doubtful whether this change was directly due to the waving of the corset, or to the nature of the speech which the dreamer was making. The comparison of the corset with a straight-waistcoat points to one aspect at least of the dreamer's attitude towards his wife being one of antagonism. It is probable that the doubtful character of the interpretation only reflects the ambivalent attitude of the patient towards his wife, his love for her being blended with antagonism due, at any rate in part, to her being one of the forces driving him back to the practice of Medicine.

The speech of the dreamer was a direct indication of a conflict which I knew to be actively present between manifest opinions that the war must be fought to a finish and deeper feelings that a struggle involving such horrors as those which he had experienced should continue. At the same time, there can be little doubt that it was also a symbolic expression of the conflict between desire to continue the work of his profession and horror at the thoughts which the practice of his profession, even in the modified form I had recommended, would inevitably arouse.

Among incidents of the dream which were readily explained by my knowledge of the patient I may mention the stress laid on the expression of agony in the eyes of the man in the audience, which was derived from a special feature of the experience with the dying French prisoner to whom I have already referred. The choice of a revolver for the suicide and the mention of the absence of blood and the fact that breathing would stop at once were also referable to this experience. The mention of the rest brought by peace and Dr X's use of the words " Angel of Peace " as an expression for " death," show clearly that the speech about the war symbolised his own struggle, with the desire for death as its end.

The two means of exit from the hall may be taken to represent the two alternative solutions of his conflict, which at the moment seemed possible ; one, the return to Medicine, symbolised by his father-in-law with his stick and snake ; the other, suicide, symbolised or represented by a person who had recently committed this act.

The impression received by the dreamer as he was beginning his speech that everyone he knew or had ever known was there, may be taken as an expression of the thought that the act then prominent in the dreamer's thoughts was one which, through the publicity attendant upon suicide, would become as prominent in the minds of all those he knew or had ever known as at the moment his place on the platform of the dream made him prominent to all those present.

This is not the place to consider the practical or the prospective value of this dream, but I may say in passing that I have never known a dream which had more important practical consequences. I was convinced at once that the mere thought of returning to Medicine, even in the modified form I had suggested, was so painful to the patient that he was contemplating suicide. When he visited me at my request I was doubtful at first whether simply to act on this conclusion without revealing my grounds for advising that he should renounce all thoughts of return to Medicine, or whether I should go into the situation with him fully. A short conversation soon made it clear that he had been entertaining definite thoughts of suicide, thoughts which had been strengthened, if not suggested, by the recent suicide of his friend, Dr X, whose rôle in the dream it was to encourage its transformed suicide. I went into the whole situation carefully with the patient, and it was decided that he should give up all thoughts of Medicine and enter upon some other career.

Having now interpreted the dream, at any rate in its main outlines, let us consider how far it supports Freud's scheme of the production and function of the dream. In the first place, the interpretation has shown that the dream was the transformed expression of a wish to commit suicide in order to escape from a conflict which was becoming intolerable. On the one side was the patient's intense desire to give up the practice of Medicine, not merely on account of anticipation of the horrors which medical practice, and especially the sight of blood, would inevitably recall, but also on account of the fears for his reason with which, in common with nearly every sufferer from the severer forms of anxiety-neurosis, the patient was troubled. On the other side of the conflict was not only the desire to please his wife's relatives as well as his own, but also the natural objection to give up a profession for the practice of which he had given many years of preparation, while combined with this was the knowledge that he had no other clear prospect of maintaining his wife and family. His love for his child was acting more explicitly perhaps than any other feature of the situation as a motive for continuing the practice of his profession.

While the dream was thus clearly the expression of a violent conflict between wishes of different kinds, it was at the same time so transformed in the dream that the patient, even after he had written out the dream and was talking about it to me, had no idea of its inner meaning. He wholly failed to recognise that the man in the audience was the dream-representative of himself. He was even unaware that the stick with the snake writhing round it was a symbol of Medicine though, even while he was talking to me about the dream, he was wearing on his tunic the badge of the R.A.M.C. Not only during the dream, but even after much consideration in the waking state, the deeper meaning of the dream was wholly hidden from him. The transformation, transparent as it seems to be, was sufficient to disguise the nature of the conflict of which his sleep had been the scene.

If we now turn to the processes which make up the dream-work, it would be difficult to find better examples of the processes of dramatisation and symbolisation. In the representation of Medicine by a snake writhing round a stick; of his wife by a corset; of the act of suicide by a recent example of this act, we have characteristic examples of symbols, while a dramatic character of the whole dream is present in an intense degree.

Of condensation the dream is full of examples, only a few of which I have been able to give, but even in the main outlines of the analysis we have in the speech of the dreamer not merely an expression of views about the war which the dreamer actually held, but the speech at the same time expressed another conflict of a wholly different kind which was also finding expression in the dream as a whole. Another example of condensation is the combination of the ancient desire to have blue eyes and of certain experiences with a French prisoner during the war, both of which contributed to make the eyes of his substitute so prominent in the dream. Again, the horror of this substitute, when threatened with the symbol of Medicine, was the expression of a large number of experiences by which this horror was produced and supported.

It is when we turn to displacement that the dream

fails to support the Freudian position. There is no question that the prominent element of the dream-thoughts was the danger of suicide. Though this act was disguised by the use of a dream-surrogate in place of the dreamer himself, suicide, disguised as homicide, was the outstanding feature of the manifest content of the dream. There was displacement in the sense that the dreamer did not direct the revolver towards himself but aimed it at his dream-representative and there was displacement in that the horror of Medicine and the love of his wife showed themselves not in himself but in the eyes, hair and face of his dream-surrogate. If, however, we understand displacement in the Freudian sense as a process in which the outstanding feature of the manifest content does not correspond with the outstanding feature of the latent content, the dream cannot be regarded as an example of the process. In this dream disguise was effected by means of symbolisation rather than by displacement.

If now we consider how far the dream is an example of wish-fulfilment, we find a situation very similar to that presented by my own dream. The patient undoubtedly wished to kill himself as a means of escaping from an intolerable situation. In waking life the patient knew that he was in danger of suicide from which, at any rate at times, he wished to be saved, and in the dream this wish was realised in a dramatic manner by the intervention of his child at the moment when the symbolic suicide was about to take place. But the dream expressed far more than this and, as in the case of my own dream, the view that this dream was a wish-fulfilment is far too simple. Again, I think there is good reason to suppose that the really important desire in the dreamer's mind was for suicide, for " the peace of death " emphasised in one passage of the dream, and that from this point of view the dream was not a fulfilment but the negation of a wish. As in the case of my own dream, it is at least equally possible to regard the dream as a whole as an attempted solution of a conflict of a very complicated kind which was going on in the mind of the dreamer, a conflict of which I have already enumerated the leading elements on either side.

Accepting, at any rate provisionally, the view that the dream was an attempted solution of a conflict, let us inquire how far it was one in which the elements found expression in forms characteristic of different periods of life. In the first place, the form in which the patient himself found expression in the dream revealed a characteristic phantasy of childhood. From childhood the patient had wished that he had blue eyes and fair hair and skin, and his appearance in the dream as a Viking was a thorough realisation of this infantile desire. The form taken by the symbolisation of Medicine was the result of a relatively late experience, but the symbolisation itself was a process of a characteristically youthful kind, though one which is frequently persistent in adult life, and especially in collective manifestations, such as heraldry and the wearing of uniforms and badges.

The act of being saved from suicide found expression in the dream through the intervention of his child, a process characteristic of the kind of melodrama which appeals to the youth, but which was of far too crude a kind to appeal to my patient in his waking state. The conflict between the deeper desire for the peace of death and the duty to live, especially for the sake of his son, was expressed in the dream by a dramatic struggle between the symbolic expressions of various factors which entered into the conflict, ending in a dramatic *dénouement* in which, at the moment of directing the revolver at his dream-substitute, he was saved by the voice of his child. The whole dream is a striking example of a process according to which the dream is a solution or attempted solution of a conflict by means of symbolic images and metaphors characteristic of different periods of life. In this case most of the symbols were of a youthful kind, but it is of great significance that there was one image which was largely devoid of this symbolic character, and was of a kind which would make a direct appeal to the adult mind. I refer to the adoption in the dream of Dr X as a representative of suicide. It is doubtful whether one would be justified in speaking of the image of Dr X as it appeared in the dream as a symbol. Dr X had committed suicide quite recently, and there is no question that when the patient was thinking of suicide in the waking state at this time, the example of Dr X was clearly in his mind. The appearance of Dr X in the manifest dream must be regarded as an example of suicide of a kind which would appeal to the adult, rather than as a symbol of suicide such as might be regarded as characteristic of childhood or youth. Though the substitution of a surrogate for himself disguised from the dreamer the fact that he was about to commit a symbolic suicide, the presence of Dr X on the stage and his obvious approval of the proposed act came nearer to the realisation of the deeper meaning of the dream than any other part of its content. I propose now to give a second dream of this patient, which may have occurred a week or two later, because it illustrates points already considered and others which I shall have to discuss later.

TRANSFERENCE DREAM

The dream was as follows :

" I was on a journey which seemed as if it would never end. I had come from a very hilly country and far back I could see many small rivers among the hills joining to form the large river by the side of which

I felt I must continue my terrible journey. I felt terribly exhausted and the river was friendly and sang to me to swim on my journey and take courage.

"I did so and felt happy and could take powerful strokes with ease and became so full of confidence that I landed and determined to walk, again keeping close by the bank of the river which I felt would help me on. Yet somehow I felt I ought to fight ahead on my own. The ground, however, was full of menace, alive with snakes, and harsh and forbidding like the desert.

"I stumbled and fell again and again, encouraged not a little by the voice of the river until I was confronted by a hideous blood-red snake reared up to strike with its tail curled round a log of dead wood. The Frenchman held it in tether round the neck by a rope which was blood.

"Then I heard my boy's voice from afar: 'Swim in the river, daddy, or he will get you,' and I knew I was so safe in the river, and yet that I would only have to leave it again to struggle on. So I determined, since I could not go on alone and could not pass the Frenchman with his awful companion to turn away into the terrible plain which was strewn with whitened bones."

This dream was of so horrible a character that the patient awoke vomiting.

The character of this dream leaves little doubt that the snake still served to symbolise Medicine and its horrors, but this meaning was more disguised than in the earlier dream by the colour of the snake and by the fact that only its tail was now connected, with the log of dead wood taking the place of the stick which more nearly resembled the caduceus of the earlier symbol. Without the presence of the symbol of the earlier dream it would have been difficult and hazardous to recognise in this image of a dream the symbol of Medicine.

C

At the same time the association of the snake of the second dream with the dying Frenchman who had come to stand in the mind of the patient for so much of his horror of Medicine only serves to confirm the conclusion that the snake was a symbol of Medicine, while "the rope of blood" brings out again the horror of blood which was connected in so many ways with the patient's dread of following his profession. We have here an elaboration of symbolism which leaves no doubt as to the meaning of the dream, though this elaboration was of a kind to disguise this meaning more fully from the sleeper.

If Medicine had been symbolised in the same way as in the earlier dream, the meaning of the symbol would have been recognised by the dreamer. Whatever may have been the basis of the elaboration of the symbolism, there can be little question that it served the function of disguising from the sleeper the meaning of his dream.

The confrontation of the dreamer with a modified form of the symbolisation of Medicine by snake and stick, however, was only an incident of the dream and not its main motive. This motive may now be considered. As soon as I heard the dream, I had no doubt that its meaning was one in which I was intimately concerned, and that it furnished another example of the capacity of my name for symbolisation or transformation. I was puzzled by the union of many small rivers to make up the large river by the side of which the dreamer was journeying, but it seems possible that this was the way in which the dream-consciousness symbolised the plural form of my name.

It is clear that the river symbolised a person or object upon whom or which the dreamer was relying for help and comfort, and there is no doubt that I stood in that relation to him. Moreover, the way in which the patient's son intervened points to my being definitely regarded by the dreamer as a protection against his being drawn back to Medicine, about which again there was no doubt. If we accept this interpretation, we have to discover why the outcome of the dream should have been that the dreamer turned away from the help which I was then offering to him.

It is necessary for this purpose that I should explain more fully the nature of my relation to the dreamer at this time. He had been my patient in Scotland, a fact which may possibly account for the hilly country with which the dream begins, and was now living in London where I was also working. At this time he could hardly be regarded as my patient. I was in touch with him as with many other of my old patients, and when I gave him the advice about taking up Public Health, it was while he was paying me a visit that I regarded merely as an occasion on which an old patient had come to talk to me about his plans for the future. As soon as I knew about the first dream, however, it became evident that the situation was far more serious than I had supposed, and I asked the patient to come to see me regularly, but he did not do so, and I accepted his own excuse that he knew I was busy and did not like to trouble me.

The second dream, however, revealed that the question of coming to see me was the subject of a serious conflict in the patient's mind, a conflict, apparently of a deep kind, between one desire to come to me for help and another desire to stand on his own 'feet and rely on his own strength. I need hardly say that it was a regular part of my treatment to guard against the process known to the psycho-analysts as transference. Though in this case there had been nothing which could properly be called psycho-analysis, I had obtained a very extensive knowledge of such parts of the patient's early experience as were accessible to consciousness without special procedures.

There had at first been rather violent resistance to this process, followed later by a state in which I had recognised the danger of transference, and it had formed an essential part of my treatment to inculcate independence, " fighting ahead on his own," to use the language of the dream. The practical importance of the dream was that it revealed a tendency to such transference so strong as to form the subject of a serious conflict, and that this conflict had acted as the basis of a dream as painful as that I have narrated.

Let us accept this interpretation, at any rate provisionally, and consider how it bears out the scheme of Freud. In the first place it is evident that while the dream readily falls into line as the attempted solution of a conflict, it is far from as readily capable of explanation by the simple formula of wish-fulfilment. If it was the fulfilment of a wish, this wish must have been that of getting away from my influence. I have no hesitation in accepting the position that this wish was present in the patient's mind and present to a degree so powerful as to lead to the occurrence of a dream of this painful kind. At the same time there was, I think, no question as to the existence of another wish, also of a powerful kind, to avoid or lessen his immediate discomforts by coming to me for help. We seem to have here a case where I believe it is far more convenient to regard the dream as a solution or attempted solution of a conflict between two powerful desires rather than the fulfilment of a wish, and I hope to show later that the adoption of the latter point of view has obscured an aspect of the dream which greatly helps us to understand its nature.

Passing to the thesis that the solution of the conflict reached or attempted by the dream is one expressed in regressive form, this dream seems to me to afford an even better example of it than either of the other dreams I have related.

My rôle in the situation with which the dreamer was presented was that of one who was protecting him from the fate of being drawn back to the practice of his profession ; and at the point which may be regarded as the crisis of the dream, he was confronted on the one hand by the symbol of Medicine, so modified as to bring into prominence the dread of blood, which had so much to do with his horror of Medicine, and on the other hand by the chance of escape by following my advice and putting all thoughts of Medicine wholly on one side. I am inclined to believe that a large element in the dream was that he was so under the influence of his family surroundings that it was almost impossible for him to follow my advice. At any rate the later history of the case points definitely in this direction.

COMPARISON OF THE THREE DREAMS

Having now described and interpreted three dreams, one of my own and two of another person, let us compare them with one another and see in what points my dream resembles or differs from the others. In all three there was such transformation of the latent meaning of the dream that its meaning was not recognised by the sleeper, but the dreams differed greatly in the amount of this transformation.

In my patient's first dream the disguise affected by the transformation of the dream was almost complete. The patient wholly failed to realise that the dream was an expression, hardly veiled at all, of the conflict which was rendering his life terrible. If it had not been for the presence of Dr X in the dream, I am doubtful whether the patient would have recognised that it bore any relation to suicide. In the patient's second dream the disguise was even more complete. In my own dream, on the other hand, I had no doubt in the dream that its subject was the choice of a President of a Society, and my act of looking to see who had been nominated as President was clearly indicative of my direct interest in the choice, though, owing to the absence of any clear limit between dream and interpretation, I am unable to say definitely whether a desire to see my own name or that of another was the explicit motive.

One important difference between my dream and the other two is thus the amount of transformation and disguise. In the dreams of my patient there was also far more symbolisation, it being through the extensive utilisation of this process that the disguise was effected. In all three dreams there was no displacement, if by displacement is meant a process in which the central point of the manifest content does not correspond with that of the latent dream-thought.

I have so far said nothing of one feature in which the examples I have described differ greatly from one another. In my own dream there was no affective accompaniment of any moment. The two dreams of my patient, on the other hand, were not only accompanied by powerful affect while they were in progress, but when he awoke from the first the dreamer felt ill and depressed and described the dream as the worst he had ever had in his life, a strong statement for one who had been troubled throughout his illness by nightmares of a fearful kind; while he awoke from the second dream in so disturbed a state that he vomited.

I propose in a later chapter to consider the problem of affect in the dream fully, and I must be content here to call attention to the great contrast in this respect between the dreams just recorded, which will provide the material for the discussion of this question,

The solution of the problem which I shall submit is that the affective character of a dream depends on whether the conflict which is finding expression in the dream receives a satisfactory solution. I suggest that when a dream provides a satisfactory solution of a conflict, the nature of which is disguised from the dreamer by a process of transformation, there is no affect, or one of slight kind, but that when the dream wholly fails to solve the situation, or still more when the solution it provides is contrary to the deepest desire of the dreamer, there is affect, and affect of a painful kind. I have suggested that the strongest motive in the conflict which produced my patient's dream was the desire for death, or rather for the peace which death would bring, a desire fitly symbolised by the reference to the Angel of Peace, emphasised by Dr X, the dream-representative of suicide. I have suggested that the highly painful character of the dream was due to the fact that this deep desire of the dreamer was frustrated by the social considerations which found concrete expression in the dream in the voice of his son. It is this point of view which has especially led me to be dissatisfied with Freud's formula of the dream as a wish-fulfilment. From my point of view this suicide-dream was not the fulfilment of a wish, but the direct negation of the wish which was at the time most prominent in the mind of the dreamer.

CHAPTER III

THE " CUP AND SAUCER " DREAM

THE first two chapters have been based on the record of dreams which were not altogether of the kind which have most excited the wonder and curiosity of students of dream-psychology. None of them can perhaps be regarded as characteristic examples of the grotesque or fantastic character which is so frequent in the consciousness of sleep. Beyond the feature that the meeting of the Council of a London Scientific Society should take place in an outhouse of a Cambridge College garden, there was nothing very fantastic about my own dream, which was mainly of an intellectual kind and devoid of any definitely affective accompaniment. The chief feature of the first dream of my patient, on the other hand, was its tragical rather than grotesque character. Though it evidently had a comic character to those who did not recognise its deeper meaning, it was far more coherent than dreams often are.

I propose now to consider another dream of my own in which the fantastic and grotesque character was definite, and to inquire whether it is possible also to lead a dream of this kind back to factors which make it intelligible and even rational.

Before I record and interpret this dream I should like to say a word about a difficulty to which I have not so far referred.

One of the greatest hindrances to the psychological study of dreams, or rather perhaps to the general discussion of its problems, is the fact that the dream is continually revealing thoughts and sentiments of the dreamer which cannot easily be made public or in which there is the risk that the object of these thoughts may be recognised. One of the infantile characters of the dream-consciousness is that it blurts out like a child just what it really thinks and feels about persons and things. Thus, in the dream of my own already recorded I was obliged to omit certain features for this reason, and the same is true of the dream which I am about to analyse.

With the dreams of others similar precautions may be even more necessary. Thus, it will be evident to all that it would be most unfortunate if the dreams utilised in the last chapter should be traced back to their source, and I have made certain alterations in the details of the dream and its interpretation which will prevent the recognition of the identity of the dreamer, but at the same time I was obliged to omit several details which would have made the interpretation even more convincing. Freud himself has suffered greatly from this limitation. As a well-known physician it is widely known who have been his patients, and this has prevented him from using much material which would doubtless have been better suited to illustrate his subject than the dreams which he has actually chosen. (In many cases of my own the interpretation would be far more convincing if it were possible to give all the facts, and if it were not necessary in many cases to omit features which would allow the identification of the subject of the dream by others.)

THE "CUP AND SAUCER" DREAM

In the dream now to be considered I was playing billiards with Dr (now Sir) Maurice Craig, the well-known specialist in mental disease. I had to make a stroke in which the place of the red ball was taken by a cup and saucer in a position relative to the white ball which would make an easy cannon, the white ball and the saucer being only a few inches from one another. I played with this intention but with a result, which I am sure neither Mr Inman nor Mr Smith could attain, that both the white ball and my own were brought into contact with the saucer and remained there. In the following stroke, which I played in spite of the fact that the balls, real or symbolic, were touching one another, I only succeeded in separating the cup and saucer from the two balls. Dr Craig then made a remark which I did not catch exactly, but I took it to be : " You should have made a two and a three of it," and as I was asking what exactly he had said, I awoke.

On thinking about the dream the first things that came into my mind were certain incidents of the previous day which had evidently determined features of the manifest content. I had dined out in the evening and my hostess had drawn my attention particularly to her coffee cups, which were of a peculiar pattern, decorated with representations of a dragon-fly. The cups had come from Sweden and the mention of the Swedish word for " dragon-fly " had formed the starting-point of a conversation on philological and ethnological topics that had greatly interested me and had given me new ideas concerning certain problems of the ethnology of northern Europe. A cup and saucer had thus formed the starting-point of a train of thought which had touched one of my chief interests. The feature which had thus determined one element of the manifest content, though apparently trivial, had in reality been closely associated with my chief interest in life.

The appearance of Dr Craig was equally natural. On the previous day I had sent him a reprint of an article, and during the evening we had spent some time watching a wonderful scene, in which Craig House stood out prominently against a background of a superb sunset. Craig House is an institution for patients with mental disorder, and would thus have strengthened the tendency already present to bring to mind a friend bearing the same name. Moreover, I was working at Craiglockhart Hospital.

The occurrence of a game of billiards as the setting of the dream was less obvious, but Dr Craig and I had been residents together at Bethlem Hospital many years ago, where we had frequently played billiards, and as he was by far the better player, I had learned much from him. His remark in the dream was altogether in keeping with his rôle as my mentor in the game.

The chief features of the manifest dream were thus capable of direct explanation through incidents of the day, and especially of the evening, immediately preceding the dream. According to the old point of view which regarded the fantastic and grotesque character of a dream as natural and as in no need of explanation, but limited this process to the manifest images of which the dream is composed, the dream would already have been analysed in a thoroughly satisfactory manner and nothing more would be needed. As I was not content with such a superficial explanation, I tried to put myself into an attitude which would allow further associations with the dream to appear, and I soon became aware of a definite visual image of one of my patients, whom I will call James, which rapidly disappeared, to be replaced by his name, which remained firmly fixed in my mind. At this time there were two patients of this name under my care. The appearance of one of them as the subject of a visual image showed that I must have been at least in a half-sleeping state, for I never experience so definite a visual image when fully awake.

The occurrence of the image and name of a patient,

either in a transient second dream, or at least in a hypnogogic state, at once brought to my mind the fact that so many of my dreams at that time had been traced to anxieties connected with my medical work, and at once two definite causes of anxiety occurred to me, one of which had presented itself when going round the hospital immediately before going to bed. The first of these two anxieties which came to my mind concerned the patient I call James, of whom I had had the visual image. He was to have a Medical Board on the following day and I had decided to recommend his return to duty. I had made a similar decision on an earlier occasion and had had to change it, owing to the appearance of new symptoms, and now that I had again decided to recommend discharge to duty, I was very doubtful whether I was taking the right course. On thinking over the situation, however, I could see no way whatever in which any conflict concerning this patient could have found expression through the symbolism of the dream. The only feature of the dream which was in any way appropriate was the intervention of Dr Craig, for the case was one in which I should have been glad of his counsel. His action as mentor at billiards was an appropriate symbol of the rôle he might have occupied as a consultant in a medical difficulty. I was wholly unable, however, to see how either the special features of the dream-game or his remark at the end bore in any way on this case. This led me to continue my search and I turned my attention to the other patient of the same name.

It is necessary here to give a preliminary account of a feature of my work at that time. The bedrooms of the hospital were small and most of them accommodated two or three patients. I was in the habit of giving much thought to the suitability to one another of patients who occupied the same room. I tried to arrange not only that they were men who would get on well together, but also that there was agreement in such points as their times of getting to sleep, their need for a light at night, and similar features of their cases. It not infrequently happened that patients put together on arrival, when little was known about them, turned out to be incongruous, and were separated, but such rearrangement could, as a rule, only take place on the days when Medical Boards were held, when vacancies made redistribution possible. As I have already mentioned, the following day was a Board-day, and we expected an unusually large number of discharges, so that there was scope for any desirable rearrangement. I had already made certain tentative plans, and on my night-round I had spoken to the Sister concerning one such rearrangement, which involved the second patient, named James, while the bed to be vacated by the first James also entered into the redistribution.

With this introduction I can return to the interpretation of the dream. When I turned my attention to the second patient named James, the whole problem concerned with my plan of redistribution came clearly to my mind and I saw that there was at least a *prima facie* case for the explanation of the game as a symbolic expression of my difficulty and its proposed solution. The second James was one of the occupants of a three-bedded room in which one of the three was disturbing another seriously by the noises he made in his sleep. My tentative solution had been to move into another room the patient who was being especially disturbed, thus separating him, not only from the patient who was disturbing him, but also from the third occupant of the room with whom he was in every way congenial. At first I considered how far the strokes of the dream-game could have symbolised my proposed distribution. It was not difficult to see that the game dealt with three objects, the two billiard balls and the cup and saucer, and that the cup and saucer might represent the patient who was disturbing the other two occupants of his room, represented by the two balls. Moreover, in a rough kind of way the result of my strokes might symbolise the aim of my proposed redistribution : for the result of the second stroke had been to separate the cup and saucer from the two billiard balls, though only after the first stroke had brought them together. At this step the remark made by Dr Craig at the end, " You should have made a two and a three of it," came into my mind. It was only when I turned my attention to this incident of the dream that a wholly new solution of the problem flashed into my mind. An event had happened on the previous day which had left a two-bedded room free and I now saw that this would enable me to move both the companions of the noisy patient instead of only one and put them together into this newly available room. At the same time I saw a means of placing the disturbing patient in such a way that it would leave me with the three-bedded room free for the use of new patients.

Dr Craig's advice in the dream-game, viz. : " You should have made a two and a three of it," seems to have given me the clue to the new arrangement. His remark is a fairly exact expression of this arrangement, for the essence of the new plan was that it enabled me to utilise a two-bedded room and leave a three-bedded room free for immediate needs, in place of the older plan for which the dream-expression had no meaning.

Though, as I have already indicated, the details of the dream-game represent more or less roughly the aims and results of the redistribution, the matter is not quite straightforward. The second stroke is comparatively simple for, if the cup and saucer symbolised the disturbing patient, it had as its result the separation of this man from the two patients whom he was dis-

‚. This separation only took place, however,
the first stroke of the game had brought them
„ether, and for this incident of the dream I can find no
very satisfactory explanation. I was more or less
responsible for these incongruous patients being together, ar˙ is possible that my responsibility in this
¬att⸢ pressed by means of the first stroke.
left with the need to explain the most
‚e of the dream, viz., the symbolisation of
ʃ means of a cup and saucer as a prominent
eie⸌ ⸴f a game of billiards. If the interpretation
which I have given is correct, it must have been the
disturbing patient who was thus symbolised, for the
whole object of the rearrangement was to separate
him from one of the other patients. We have to
discover why this patient should have been represented in this grotesque fashion. Though the chief
reason for separating the patient from one of his companions was that he slept badly, only got to sleep late
at night, and then was so noisy and restless that he
disturbed the sleep of his companions, and especially
the second James, he was also thoroughly incompatible
with the other occupants of his room in interests.
The disturbing patient was a man who seemed to be
devoid of any of the qualifications usually regarded as
those of an officer in the army. So far as one could
see, he possessed neither the intellectual or social
qualities nor the force of character which would fit
him for the position. He seemed, indeed, as much
out of place as an officer in the army as a cup and
saucer is unfitted to serve as the object of a stroke at
billiards.

At the same time the social disqualification of
this patient for his position helps to explain another
difficulty. Though I had a certain amount of anxiety
about this rearrangement, it was an anxiety of a wholly
altruistic kind. I mistrust any interpretation of a

dream which does not lead one back to a factor which definitely touches the self-interest of the dreamer and makes the conflict upon which the dream depends one which affects himself. If the problem with which we are dealing had been one which merely concerned the health and comfort of patients, I am doubtful whether it would have formed the basis of a dream. Is it possible, then, that there were factors in this case which would have led to the presence of an egoistic aspect ? It was not difficult to find such an aspect, one directly referable to the personality and social position of the disturbing patient. As soon as I turned my attention to this aspect of the case, I was aware that I had been the subject of a definite conflict, owing to the doubt whether I was not being influenced in my decision to separate two patients by other than purely medical considerations. I believed that the health of one of the patients was being prejudiced by association with so bad a sleeper, but at the same time I could not help fearing that I might also be influenced by the social incompatibility of the two men, and was laying myself open, at any rate in my own mind, to the suspicion of favouritism. I believe that this motive, one directly connected with those qualities of the disturbing patient which makes his representation as a cup and saucer appropriate, introduced just that egoistic element which was necessary to make the interpretation complete.

It is also of importance that my former plan was one which would have made it possible for the disturbing patient to suspect that separation from himself was the motive of the change, whereas the new plan formulated as the result of the dream was less open to this possibility.

I have now finished the interpretation of the dream, but before I proceed to consider it in its theoretical bearings, I should like to say that I shall quite understand the scepticism if anyone hesitates to accept the interpretation. To my mind it is almost too good to be true and is one of those cases in which you are justified in thinking that the case is so good that there must be something wrong with it. Though I cannot help sharing these doubts myself, I propose to accept the interpretation provisionally and as a basis for the discussion of certain theoretical problems.

I will begin with one which so far we have not touched, viz., the function of the dream as a constructive agency. It is well known that novelists, of whom Stevenson is perhaps the most striking instance, have utilised dreams in the construction of their plots, and dreams have also taken a definite part in the production of poetry. The experience I have just recorded suggests that the dream may also be capable of solving or helping to solve such practical problems as are presented by the course of daily life and, though in fantastic form, may express conclusions better than those reached by the waking consciousness. In the case I have related it would appear that the dream-consciousness utilised a piece of information, viz., the setting free of a two-bedded room, the importance of which had not been grasped by the consciousness of the waking life.

If my interpretation is correct, we have here a definite contribution to the evidence upon which it may some day be possible to formulate a scheme of the constructive function of the dream. I have shown reason to believe that this dream was the expression of a conflict between the necessities of certain patients and the fear of laying myself open to the charge of favouritism, and if this were so, the dream was not merely a solution of the conflict, but a successful solution, a solution better than that which I had reached when awake. It is not necessary to modify our tentative conclusion that the dream is the solution of a conflict, but it is desirable to consider once again why the solution reached by the dream should find expression in a fantastic or even grotesque form, which not only disguised its meaning from the sleeper, but made it far from easy to recognise this meaning even after waking. While it is possible to see why it may be at least serviceable that the meaning of a dream should be disguised when it is unpleasant, or reveals features of the sleeper's mental make-up, of which he might be ashamed, it is difficult to see why there should also be disguise of such a constructive function as seems to have been present in the dream which I have related.

If, however, I am right in my supposition that the protective function of the dream is a secondary feature and that the disguise of the dream is a necessary consequence of its infantile character, or at least of its character as an expression of the mentality of some period of life earlier than that of the occurrence of the dream, the difficulty disappears. The disguise of the practical and constructive value of the dream, though of no service, or rather of disservice to the dreamer, is a necessary consequence of the essential nature of the dream as the coming into being of an early form of mental functioning. The form in which the constructive function of the dream manifests itself only serves to support a conclusion reached by the study of dreams in which no such constructive function can be detected.

Returning now to the inquiry how far the billiard dream serves to illustrate points already dealt with in Chapters I and II, we have already seen how it supports the view that dreams are solutions of conflicts. In this case again the Freudian interpretation that the dream is a wish-fulfilment is too crude and simple a statement of the case. It might be possible to state the case as one in which the dream was the fulfilment of a wish to carry out a certain purpose without exposing myself to the charge of favouritism, but I believe it is a far more suitable view to regard the dream as the solution of a conflict, a conflict of a rather complex kind. Still more important is the problem why this conflict, which was of no especially unpleasant kind, should have found expression in the fantastic and grotesque imagery which formed so effectual a disguise. In my opinion it is quite unnecessary to have recourse to the concept of an agency watching at the threshold of consciousness which only allowed this conflict to reach consciousness in this disguised form. It is enough for me that the dream, being a regressive phenomenon, seized upon objects to which my attention had been drawn the evening before and chose them to form symbols of the person round whom the conflict centred, and of the setting in which the conflict was symbolically solved. The process of symbolisation illustrated in this dream is absolutely foreign to all my normal adult modes of mental functioning when awake, and I can only suppose that at one period of my life I was accustomed to think in such images.

I can now turn to consider how far the dream I have just recorded illustrates the different processes by which the meaning of a dream finds expression in manifest form. It is not necessary to dwell on the value of this dream as an example of the processes of dramatisation and symbolisation, and I can pass at once to the feature of condensation. Here I must begin by referring to a feature of the dream and its interpretation which I have hitherto left on one side. I may remind you that the starting-point of the interpretation was the appearance, either in a second dream or as a hypnogogic hallucination, of the image of a patient who had the same name as a man who entered into a situation which seems to have formed the real central point of the dream. So far as I could tell, my anxiety about this patient was considerably greater than that involved in the problem concerning the re-arrangement of bedrooms, and the appearance of an image of this patient during the process of interpretation suggests that the anxiety about him may have helped in the determination of the dream, even though his case seems to have had nothing to do with the imagery of the dream itself.

The combination of the sending of a reprint to Dr Craig and the view of Craig House may also be regarded as an example of condensation in determining the manifest content of the dream.

So far as displacement is concerned, the dream seems to confirm the conclusion based on the dreams already considered. The whole process of interpretation points to a problem in which an incongruous patient was the central personage of the latent dream-thoughts and of his separation from his companions the essential object of these thoughts. On the other hand, the cup and saucer and their separation in the dream-game from the billiard balls were also the prominent features of the manifest dream. The dream gives no support whatever to the occurrence of displacement in Freud's sense, viz., as a process in which elements prominent in the latent content become of subsidiary importance in the manifest dream.

The appearance of the image of the first James during the process of interpretation would seem to be a far better example of displacement. This displacement, however, was not a feature of the original dream, but of an occurrence which was either a second dream or a hypnogogic hallucination which occurred in the course of the interpretation. The dream I just have related agrees with those already considered in showing that symbolisation plays a far more active part in effecting disguise than the process of displacement, or at any rate that kind of displacement upon which Freud lays especial stress.

CHAPTER IV

METHODS OF DREAM-ANALYSIS *

THERE can be no doubt that the conditions under which dreams are recorded and analysed have a great influence upon the results obtained in the analysis. Thus, the doctrines concerning dreams held by Freud, Jung and psycho-analysts generally are greatly affected by the fact that most of the dreams they analyse and make the basis of their theoretical views are obtained in the course of psycho-analysis, *i.e.* in the course of a long-continued process of a complex and peculiar kind in which there is a special relation, again of a peculiar kind, between the person whose dreams are being analysed and the person who is performing the analysis. Freud has even shown reason to believe † that some of the dreams of his patients have been the outcome of a wish on their part that the views on which their treatment is being based should be shown to be wrong. If factors, such as resistance to the views of the analyst, which enter into the process of psycho-analysis can have an effect of this crude kind, we can be confident that influences of a far more subtle kind, influences less easily detected, must be continually in action, and that, on the whole, the influence of psycho-analysis will be to produce dreams which will tend to confirm the views of those conducting the analysis. We

* This chapter was read at a General Meeting of the British Psychological Society on 23rd July 1921, and published in *The British Journal of Psychology* (*Medical Section*), Vol. II, Part 2, January 1922, the Editor of which has kindly consented to its reproduction here.
† *Die Traumdeutung*, 5te Auflage, Leipzig and Wien, 1919, pages 104 and 106 (Brill's translation, page 127).

can have little doubt, for instance, that an analyser who believes, or who is generally supposed to believe, that all psycho-neuroses, if not all dreams, are due to disturbance of the sexual instinct will through this belief, or supposed belief, influence the dreams of his patients and, if he is known to hold this belief, he will produce this effect even if he is careful not to refer to sex in any way in the course of his analysis. It is therefore by no means strange that such a physician as Stekel, who believes that the context of nearly all dreams is sexual * and evidently discusses this belief with his patients, should find sexual motives so prominent in their dreams. We can also be confident that one who is believed by his patients, or his prospective patients, to hold this belief will have a similar effect even if he says or does nothing wittingly during the analysis to confirm the belief. At the same time the converse must be true. There is the similar danger that analyses of dreams which take place under the dominant influence of one who disbelieves, or is supposed to disbelieve, in the influence of sex will tend to give results in accordance with this attitude, or supposed attitude, of the analyser.

Again, if wishes concerning the truth or falsity of a theory can have the effect on the dreams of patients which Freud supposes, how far-reaching must be the effects which such wishes must have upon the dreams of one who has formulated a theory or has adopted with fervour the theory of another. The self-analysis of dreams must be exposed in equal or even greater measure to the possibility of influences tending to produce dreams which support, or can be utilised in support of, the theory which is dominating the dreamer.

Equally important must be the conditions under which dreams are analysed after they have occurred. It must make a great difference whether the dream is

* *Die Sprache des Traumes*, Wiesbaden, 1911, page 13.

analysed at once or after an interval of hours or days; whether the analysis is carried out by the dreamer himself or by another; whether the incidents of the dream are remembered and recorded before the analysis begins or whether they are only brought to light in the course of the analysis; whether the associations with the dream are left wholly open, whether they start from different selected elements of the manifest content, and whether they are assisted by some special process of word-association. Lastly, and perhaps most important of all, it must make a great difference in the case of analysis by other than the dreamer to how great an extent the analyser intervenes in the process of analysis and tends, perhaps even unwittingly, to direct the course of the thoughts to which the analysis leads.

If dream-analysis is exposed to all these sources of error, and we may take it as certain that their influence cannot be excluded, it becomes of the utmost importance that one who utilises dreams in the study of psychological problems should make it his business to record as fully as possible the conditions under which the dreams he studies have been experienced, recorded and analysed. It becomes equally important that those engaged in the study of dreams should consider fully different methods of record and analysis and should seek to discover procedures which will at least reduce to as small proportions as possible the various sources of error to which dream-analysis is open.

As I am at present engaged in such an attempt to utilise an extensive record both of my own dreams and of the dreams of others, I propose to employ this opportunity in giving an account of my own procedure together with a criticism of the procedure now in vogue among psycho-analysts as a means of producing criticism of my own procedure and counter-criticism of my remarks on the procedure of others.

METHODS OF DREAM-ANALYSIS

In describing my own procedure it is necessary to begin with a feature of my own general psychological experience which has an important bearing on my method of analysing dreams.

For many years I have been the habitual subject of an experience in which, as soon as I become aware that I am awake, I find that I am thinking, and have for some time been thinking, over some problem, usually in connection with the scientific work upon which I am at the time engaged. Many of the scientific ideas which I value most, as well as the language in which they are expressed, have come to me in this half-sleeping, half-waking state directly continuous with definite sleep. When I began to analyse my dreams I frequently had a similar experience in which as soon as I was awake I found that I was already having, and had for some time been having, thoughts about a dream, the dream itself being still clearly in my mind. In some cases it was difficult to say where the dream ended and the unwitting analysis had begun, but a distinction was usually possible owing to my lack of imagery when awake.* I could be confident that so long as the experience was accompanied by definite imagery it was that of a dream or of a dream-like state, while the period when imagery was absent was one in which I was no longer dreaming, though I had not yet realised that I was awake.

This peculiarity of my experience of the process of awaking introduces a special feature into the records and analyses of my own dreams. There can be little question that the ideal condition for an irreproachable analysis of a dream is one in which the dream is fully recorded before the analysis begins. In this case all danger is avoided that elements derived from, or suggested by, the analysis may be incorporated into the tissue of the dream. In many cases in which I awoke

* See *Instinct and the Unconscious*, Cambridge, 1920, page 11.

from a dream more or less suddenly I was able to fulfil this ideal condition, but in the frequent cases in which the dream passed insensibly into the half-waking, half-sleeping and unwitting process of analysis, the danger to which I have referred cannot be excluded. The comparison of dreams so analysed, or partially so analysed, with those where the act of awaking was sudden shows, however, that there is little or no difference between them, and I am inclined to regard my unwitting or partially unwitting method of analysis as one especially likely to lead one to the real thoughts and emotions forming the latent content of the dream.

In other cases, after having fully awaked and recorded the dream, I would fall into the half-waking, half-sleeping state, and not infrequently it was in this state that the thoughts came which furnished the explanation of the dream. In more than one case this later period of sleepiness passed into one which must be regarded as sleep, for the clue to the nature of the dream came as a definite image. In these cases we may regard the interpretation of a dream as having been furnished by a second dream even though, as matter of fact, this second dream may have consisted only of a single image.

Where the solution of the dream failed to come in this more or less spontaneous way, I adopted the more usual procedure of turning my attention to different elements of the manifest content, allowing any associations so aroused to pass through my mind. I also searched the experience of the day or two before the dream which could have taken part in determining the nature of the manifest content and in some cases found that the experience which had determined the manifest content was of distinct service in the process of finding the deeper meaning of the dream. When I had reached what seemed to me to be the interpretation of the dream I wrote out the analysis as fully as possible and except in a few cases, the exceptions being definitely noted in my records, the complete analysis of the dream had been made and recorded before breakfast on the morning immediately following the dream.

When features of the dream come to mind during the process of analysis I am accustomed to indicate their late coming to mind by enclosing them in brackets, and similarly when elements are added to the analysis after it has been first written out, this is indicated in a similar manner.

So far as I am aware, we have few records of the methods adopted when dreams have been analysed by the dreamers themselves, but so far as can be judged from chance remarks, the method appears in general to be similar to that by which it is customary, and usually necessary, to analyse the dreams of others. At some period of the day following the dream, the dreamer takes different elements of the manifest content and allows his thoughts to rove freely from these starting-points and notes the images and ideas which come into his mind. In other words he imitates as closely as possible the method of free association which it is customary to employ when analysing the dreams of others. We are not told whether the dream is written out before the analysis begins and any further additions clearly distinguished from those already recorded, though it is occasionally mentioned that a feature of the dream only came to mind during the process of analysis. This point is of great importance in relation to the category of secondary elaboration of which so much use is made by Freud in his theoretical discussions of the dream.

I can now pass to the methods which I have adopted in analysing the dreams of others. I have rarely adopted the usual psycho-analytic procedure in which the patient is made to lie down in the presence of the analyser and started by him upon the process of free association, for I believe that in the majority of persons a state of a hypnoidal kind is thus set up which greatly assists the occurrence of a process of morbid transference. In some cases where I was already well acquainted with the special desires and anxieties of the dreamer the main lines of analysis were already clear as soon as the dream had been related. In such cases I endeavoured by means of guarded inquiries, carefully avoiding leading questions, to ascertain whether this interpretation was justified, and frequently these conversations led me to discover new wishes and anxieties or modifications of those with which I was already acquainted.

In other cases in which the dreamer has adopted a procedure on waking, similar to that followed by myself, I have obtained valuable clues to the meaning of a dream. My method in these cases has been to instruct the patient as far as possible in my own procedure and to make the analysis a matter in which the patient and I are partners.

Before proceeding further I may say that in the majority of cases this process of analysis has led me to wishes, anxieties and conflicts arising out of recent experience which have served to explain, not only the general features of the dream, but also its details. I am ready to acknowledge that a deeper and longer analysis would in many cases have led to earlier and deeper experience, while there can, in my opinion, be no doubt that when the experience of early years has been brought to the surface, or is in course of being brought to the surface during an analysis, desires and conflicts arising out of this experience contribute to the full interpretation of the dream. It seems to me, however, necessary that we should distinguish carefully between certain differences in the subject-matter of dreams which are often confused.

In dealing with this subject I will begin by considering how far the material reached by the customary process of free association can legitimately be held to have taken a necessary part in the causation of the dream. The assumption which underlies the whole construction of Freudian dream-analysis is that the process of free association, starting from an element of the manifest content of a dream, will lead to the discovery of experience which enters into the chain of causation by which the dream has been produced.

I am quite ready to acknowledge that this process leads the analyst to experience which enables him to understand the state, morbid or otherwise, of the person who is being analysed, and since in many cases this state may have taken part in determining the nature of the dream, the process will, in these cases, give valuable indications of the conditions by which the dream has been produced. It is, however, a purely arbitrary assumption to suppose that every element of experience to which one is led by the process of free association has had a share in the production of the dream except in the very broad sense that behaviour at any moment, waking or sleeping, is determined by the sum total of the experience of the behaver. Every feature of experience to which one is led by the process of free association may have contributed to the causation of the dream, but it is a pure assumption, and one which needs far firmer foundations than have been provided by the psycho-analysts, that the experience to which free association leads has the importance universally attached to it by the psycho-analytic school.

Except for the practical reason already mentioned, I have no fault to find with the process of free association as an instrument of diagnosis and treatment, or as a means of contributing to the better understanding of the mind or behaviour of the person whose dreams are being analysed, but I need far more evidence than

we possess at present to satisfy me that the process
of free association starting from an incident of a dream
necessarily leads one to experience which has taken
any direct part in the causation of the dream, and
these doubts become all the stronger, the greater the
interval between the dream and the analysis.

I am ready to acknowledge that the special conditions under which dreams are utilised by psycho-
analysts should lead to some degree, and perhaps to a
considerable degree, of relation between the elements of
a dream and experience to which one is led by the
process of free association starting from those elements.
When the practice of psycho-analysis is in progress
from day to day, it is only natural that elements which
enter into the causation of dreams should also enter
into the chains of association which emerge when an
element of a dream is taken as a starting-point. I
wish to make clear that I am not objecting to the use
of associations starting from an incident of a dream as
a process of diagnostic value, while I concede that the
special conditions under which dreams are usually
analysed by psycho-analysts will probably lead to
the presence of a relation, if not a directly causal relation, between an incident of a dream and experience to
which the dreamer, starting from that incident, is led
by free association.* My point is one of scientific
rather than of practical method. I am objecting to
the view that experience reached by free association
starting from an incident of a dream has any necessary connection with the dream, and I believe that the
chance of any such connection is especially slight
where only a single dream is analysed, or where the
interpretation of a dream does not form part of a long-
continued process of psycho-analysis.

The criticism which I am now making of the cus-

* In this case the time-interval between dream and analysis will
be of no great importance.

tomary psycho-analytic method of dream-analysis has been foreseen and answered by Freud,* but the answer seems to me far from satisfactory. It reveals a failure to appreciate the difference between the value of free association as a method of psycho-analysis, *i.e.* as a method of practical diagnosis, and its value as an instrument in the scientific study of the dream. Freud answers the objection I am now making by referring to the congruity of the results reached by the method and their agreement with the results of the treatment of hysterical symptoms, in which case he regards the disappearance of these symptoms as evidence for the correctness of the procedure. He then launches out into a defence of his method against a charge, very different from mine, that the chain of association is arbitrary and not strictly determined, and he repels the concept of a chain of thought without a definite end. He assumes that in the process of dream-analysis, this end is necessarily that which has determined the nature and course of the dream.

I have already mentioned one factor which is present whenever the dream of one person is analysed by another. In this case a person takes a part in determining the chain of associations who was not necessarily influential in determining the course of the dream. In this case I am very far from denying that the process of free association is strictly determined. I am only being more thorough in my belief in determinism in that I am including the activity of the analyser, whether witting or unwitting, in the process of determination.

Even when the dream is analysed by the dreamer himself, in which case this extraneous element in the process of determination has been excluded, it is

* *Die Traumdeutung*, 5te Auflage, Leipzig and Wien, 1919, page 393 (Brill's translation, page 418) ; also *Vorlesungen zur Einführung in die Psychoanalyse*, Leipzig and Wien, 1916, page 108.

wholly unjustifiable to conclude that thoughts reached by the process of free association have necessarily taken a part in determining the dream. It is necessary here to distinguish between two cases, that in which the associations are formed in the fully waking state and that in which they occur in the half-waking or hypnoidal state. In the former case it is evident that factors will be present during the process of association which were not present in the determination of the dream, and these additional factors will probably be the more numerous and more influential, the greater the interval between the occurrence of the dream and the time of its analysis. If, on the other hand, self-analysis takes place in the half-waking or hypnoidal state, it becomes far more probable that there will be a relation between the thoughts reached by the process of association and those which have determined the dream, but even here we cannot be absolutely confident that the associations will retrace exactly the path which they had previously followed when, according to hypothesis, they were determining the dream. If a period of wakefulness and witting reflection has been allowed to intervene between the dream and the process of analysis, no believer in strict determinism can arbitrarily reject this period as having played no part in the process by which the later associations have been determined, and the chance that this period has had an effect is the greater, the less free the process of analysis is left and the more the self-analyser adopts the artificial method of directing his thoughts to different elements of the manifest dream. The objection I bring against Freud's method of dream-analysis by free association is that it neglects factors which must be acknowledged to play a part if the doctrine of determinism is to hold good. The thoughts associated with a dream are the more likely to lead back to those by which the dream was determined, the more influences of other kinds can be excluded and the less the degree in which witting processes are allowed to intervene. It is for that reason that I believe the orthodox psycho-analytic method to be unsatisfactory and the method by which I have analysed my own dreams to be that best fitted to bring out the nature of the latent content. I have already mentioned that this method may fail to reach a solution and that in such case success may nevertheless be attained by the use of the method of free association starting from incidents of the dream. Moreover, analysis by another person may succeed where self-analysis has failed. I do not regard my own method as infallible or of universal application, but as one which is free from certain sources of error which must accompany the application of the orthodox psycho-analytic procedure. The assumption upon which my method depends is that the latent thoughts which have determined the nature of a dream during sleep continue to be active on awaking, especially when this waking is only partial, and that the period between sleeping and waking provides the fittest opportunity for the discovery of these thoughts.

CHAPTER V

AFFECT IN THE DREAM *

In the second chapter I pointed out that the dreams which I had chosen to introduce the subject differed greatly in their affective character, my own manifest dream being apparently devoid of any affect, while the dreams of my patient were of so unpleasant a kind that he described one as the most terrible he had ever known and vomited on waking from the other. I propose now to consider the relation of affect to the dream more fully, and will begin with Freud's view concerning this relation. According to Freud one character of the dream is that its manifest content is as a rule poorer in affect than the dream-thoughts. Where there is an affect in the manifest dream it will also be found in the latent content, but the converse is not true. There may be no appreciable affective disturbance in the manifest dream when the presence of affect in the deeper content is evident. In other words, one of the results of the transformation of the latent into the manifest content of the dream is not only to disguise the nature of the dream-thoughts from the sleeper, but also to lessen or inhibit its affective character ; and just as Freud ascribes the fact of disguise to the censorship, so does he ascribe to this agency the lessening or inhibition of affect. I will begin by saying that my own experience definitely confirms Freud's statement that affect may be absent or at

* This chapter was published in the *British Journal of Psychology* (General Section), Vol. XII, Part 2, in October 1921, and is reproduced here with the permission of the Editor.

E

least inappreciable in the manifest dream when it is evidently present in the deeper dream-thoughts of which the manifest dream is the transformed expression. This is a definite fact which has to be explained by any theory which endeavours to account for the relation of the dream to the affective aspect of experience. I propose, however, to begin the consideration of this subject by dealing with a variety of the dream in which affect is not merely present in the manifest content, but is present in an extreme degree. In the nightmare there is painful affect of the most intense kind, and any theory of the dream must take account of this character. This variety of dream, in the form of so-called night-terror, is especially liable to occur in childhood, but examples of one kind or another often occur in adult life, especially under abnormal circumstances. Everyone who had to do with war-neurosis became very familiar with this form of dream as a characteristic example of the nightmare.

The nightmare of war-neurosis generally occurred at first as a faithful reproduction of some scene of warfare, usually some experience of a particularly horrible kind or some dangerous event, such as a crash from an aeroplane. A characteristic feature of this variety of dream is that it is accompanied by an affect of a peculiarly intense kind, often with a special quality described as different from any known in waking life. The dream ends suddenly by the patient waking in a state of acute terror directly continuous with the terror of the dream and with all the physical accompaniments of extreme fear, such as profuse sweating, shaking, and violent beating of the heart. Often the dream recurs in exactly the same form night after night, and even several times in one night, and a sufferer will often keep himself from sleeping again after one experience from dread of its repetition.

Two of these features are of special interest in relation

to the place of affect in the dream. One is that the affective disturbance is extreme in amount ; the other, that the dream is often the repetition of an actual experience without transformation of any kind. There is absolutely nothing of the grotesque or fantastic, but the dream follows the grim reality faithfully. Moreover, it is often in my experience one of the first signs of improvement that some amount of transformation appears ; the events of the actual experience are replaced in the dream by incidents of other kinds, such as the appearance of terrifying animals, which stand in no direct relation to the actual war-experience of the dreamer. Though in these cases the dream continues to be accompanied by fear, this is less intense and accompanied by less severe physical manifestations, and in many cases this transformed character serves as a stage towards the disappearance of the " nightmare " character of the dreams. The course of many of these cases suggests that there is a definite relation between the amount of transformation and the intensity of the affect. They suggest that the intensity of affect is inversely proportional to the amount of transformation, a suggestion in harmony with the view of Freud that one of the results of the transformation of the latent into the manifest content of the dream is to lessen or inhibit its affective character.

When, however, we examine these dreams more closely we find that they show features which can hardly be reconciled with the general Freudian position. Above all is the difficulty of reconciliation with the view that every dream is a wish-fulfilment. It is difficult to see how such awful and terrifying experiences as those of dreams of this kind can be the result of wishes of the dreamer. Even if there were no other facts to lead us to regard Freud's view that the dream is a wish-fulfilment as unduly simple, and in my opinion there are many such facts, the nightmare and the battle-dream would themselves be sufficient to lead us to revise the Freudian view. In its place I am accustomed to look upon the dream as the attempted solution of a conflict, an attempt to solve a conflict of the waking life by such means as still remain open when the higher levels of mental activity have been put out of action by the inhibition of sleep.

Following this line of thought let us inquire how far the nightmare and the battle-dream are capable of explanation as infantile attempts to solve a conflict. In considering this matter I will begin with a feature of dreams of this kind which I have not so far mentioned.

In most, if not all, battle-dreams it is found that in the waking state the dreamer has been striving to keep out of his consciousness the experience which is reproduced in the dream. He has been repressing this experience. It has been found over and over again that when this process of repression is given up, the dreams no longer occur, or, if they continue, lose their terrifying character. A large body of evidence accumulated during the later years of the war shows that these terrifying dreams are due to repression of the experience which forms the content of the dream. So far as desire enters into causation, the dream is the direct negation of a wish, the wish not to be subjected to the repetition of a painful experience, the wish leading to a process of repression in the waking life which in its turn produces the dream in sleep.

Taking the process as a whole it seems to have the following character : One who has dreams of this kind has been the subject of a painful experience which tends to obtrude itself upon his attention, a tendency which is counteracted by a process of repression, a process of keeping the experience out of attention whenever it tends to appear. The conflict is one between a process in which an experience tends to recur to memory and a desire that the experience shall not recur. So long as the subject of this conflict is awake, the process of repression has the upper hand, but as soon as sleep occurs and the procèss of witting repression is removed, the repressed experience meets with no obstacle and makes its presence felt with full force. From this point of view the dream, instead of being the fulfilment of a wish, conscious or unconscious, is the complete failure of a wish which is only effectual so long as the subject of the experience remains awake. The experience of the nightmare not only fails wholly to fit into the category of wish-fulfilment ; it suggests that this form of dream is essentially an expression of the complete negation of a wish.

If now we turn to consider how far a dream of this kind can be regarded as the solution of a conflict, we find that a conflict is undoubtedly present, viz., a conflict between the tendency of an experience to recur and the wish that it shall not do so. But if the dream is regarded as a solution of this conflict, it is a solution of a quite unsuccessful kind, so far as the health and happiness of the dreamer is concerned. From this point of view a dream of this kind must be regarded as a failure of solution, and, if I am right in my view concerning the dependence of this form of dream upon repression, a failure directly due to a wrong method of meeting the situation. The whole process belongs to a category of a kind very different from that in which we place dreams of the more usual kind.

In the case, on the other hand, in which the dream begins to show a certain amount of transformation with the accompaniment of less intense affect, we find ourselves in the presence of a process of the same order as that with which we are acquainted in dreams of the customary kind. It is only when the process of transformation begins that it becomes at all possible to consider the nightmare as the solution of a conflict, and since in this case the chief result at first is to lessen the intensity of the painful affect, it can only be regarded as a solution of an imperfect kind, the effect of the transformation being to lessen to some extent the painfulness of an experience which the dreamer wishes to keep altogether out of his consciousness. If we include the nightmare in the dream-category, it becomes no longer possible simply to regard the dream as the solution of a conflict, though it may still be possible to look upon it as an attempted solution. It is to the process of transformation that we must look as the instrument whereby the dream-consciousness reaches a symbolic solution of a conflict which is present both in the sleeping and the waking mind.

The nightmare, especially in the pure form taken by the battle-dream, has such special characters that it might perhaps seem desirable to exclude it from the category of dreams and put it in a class by itself. If, however, such a suggestion were seriously entertained, it would be necessary to point out that the same need arises in the case of dreams of a very different kind. There is a large class of dreams, that with a manifest sexual content, in which there may be little or no transformation and the affective accompaniment is of a pleasant kind. Moreover, the affect may be present in an intense degree and accompanied by physical manifestations just as appropriate to the content as sweating and tremor are appropriate to the dream dependent on fear. Another point of similarity between the two kinds of dream is that the manifest sexual dream is almost certainly connected with repression and can be lessened in frequency and intensity, or altogether inhibited, if the repression ceases. Here, again, there is reason to believe that when transformation occurs in this class of dream, it is associated with a lessening or disappearance of affect. If the absence of transformation is to exclude from the dream-category, the process of exclusion will have to go far beyond the nightmare and will apply to frequent experiences of sleep which are universally recognised as dreams.

The study of the nightmare with its excess of affective disturbance has thus far led us to connect affect with the degree of transformation and to regard lessening or total inhibition of affect as a function of the process of transformation rather than of the dream process in general. Moreover, we are led to regard the nightmare as a phenomenon of sleep in which the affective disturbance is of an extremely painful kind because the dream is the expression of complete failure in a conflict, a conflict between the tendency for a painful experience to recur and an intense desire that it shall not do so. We are tempted to connect the extremely painful character of the affective disturbance with the complete failure of the dream as the solution of a conflict. It is suggested that whether a dream is accompanied by a painful affect, or has an indifferent character from the affective aspect, depends on the degree of success in the solution of the conflict which is finding expression. The general view is suggested that where a conflict is solved in a dream in a symbolic manner there is no affect.

Thus, in the two dreams of my own, we must suppose that there was no appreciable affect, because these dreams were satisfactory solutions of the conflicts upon which they depended. In the Presidency dream (Chapter I) the solution was a compromise between conflicting desires which satisfied both parties to the conflict, while the " cup and saucer " dream (Chapter III) was even more satisfactory in that it furnished, though in symbolic guise, a solution even more satisfying than that previously reached by the waking consciousness. But where the solution is completely unsuccessful there is affect of a highly painful kind ; and that different degrees of painfulness of the affect depend on different degrees in which the dream forms a successful solution.

According to this point of view a dream is accompanied by a painful affect because it fails to provide a solution of the conflict upon which the dream depends, and when there is transformation in the dream the degree of painfulness of the accompanying affect is correlated with the extent to which the dream provides a solution of this conflict. I have considered the typical battle-dream as an example of the case in which there is a complete failure of solution, and it remains to give examples of cases in which, though the dream is accompanied by transformation, this fails to provide a solution of the conflict upon which the dream depends.

One such example is the highly painful dream of a patient reported in Chapter II, which was found to arise out of a situation of a very difficult and unpleasant kind. In the final incident the dreamer was about to shoot a dream-personage, who was certainly a surrogate of himself, when he was stopped by the voice of his child saying : " Don't do it, daddy, you'll hurt me too." The dreamer was at the time involved in a very severe conflict between a desire on the one hand for suicide and for the peace which that act would bring, and on the other, motives of a social kind which acted in the opposite direction, prominent among these being the knowledge that every suicide inflicts a social stigma upon those he leaves behind him. The dream ended with the victory of these latter motives as expressed in the voice of his son, and the consequent frustration of the wish for the solution of the conflict which would bring rest and peace.

In the other dream of the same patient, the " transference dream " of Chapter II, which was so unpleasant that he awoke vomiting, the dream ended by his turning away into a wilderness from a river which was shown by the analysis to symbolise myself. The dream expressed a conflict between his tendency to undue reliance upon my help and his desire to stand on his own feet, and the ending of the dream expressed a frustration of his wish to continue to rely on me for help and comfort. The dream had its source in a situation arising out of the process of " transference " in the course of psycho-therapy.

Both these dreams support the conclusion reached by the study of the battle-dream that the affective accompaniment of the dream is determined by the degree in which the dream reaches a satisfactory solution of the conflict upon which it depends. The extreme affect of the nightmare, according to this view, will be the result of the complete failure to effect a solution, while the highly painful character of the two dreams of my patient was due to the dream-consciousness having reached a solution contrary to the desires most prominent and most potent in the sleeper's consciousness when awake.

Having reached this solution of our problem, I can now consider another aspect of the dream so far as its affective nature is concerned. According to the view here put forward, dreams are not only regarded as solutions of conflicts, but as solutions of a kind differing from those adopted in healthy waking life in that the solution has an infantile character,* or at least a character belonging to a period of life earlier than that of the occurrence of the dream. Let us now inquire how far this infantile character is true of the nightmare, again taking the war-dream as our instance. The first point to notice is that under the ordinary circumstances of our modern civilised life, dreams of this character are exceptional in the adult. It is in childhood that they are best known, forming the basis of the night-terrors from which so many children suffer. When they occur in the adult, they may be regarded as

* See *Instinct and the Unconscious*, page 230.

73

examples of regression to a state characteristic of childhood.

A feature of the war-dream, and of other adult nightmares, is the exaggerated character of the fear experienced, this exaggeration being again a character of infancy and childhood. There is little doubt that infancy and childhood form a period of life in which the human being is liable to affective disturbances of a very intense kind with the crude explosive nature which is characteristic of the affect of the nightmare or war-dream.

Still another feature of the war-dream, and probably also of the adult nightmare in general, is of special significance. The affective disturbance is described as having a peculiar quality unlike any experience of adult waking life, or only paralleled by the gusts of unreasoning terror which are also liable occasionally to overwhelm sufferers from certain forms of psychoneurosis. It is not, of course, possible to say that this quality which seems so peculiar and strange to the adult is a regression to a quality of the fears of childhood, but this is at least possible.

I suggest, therefore, that the nightmare and the war-dream are themselves examples of infantile states, that they are occurrences of the sleep of adults which appear in a form characteristic of infancy.

If now we pass to the stage of the war-dream in which transformation appears, one of the most frequent forms in which this transformation shows itself in my experience is that terrifying animals take the place of the incidents of warfare which have hitherto formed the exclusive content of the dream. There is little question that animals are prominent in the terrifying dreams of childhood, and their occurrence in the transformed war-dream may thus be regarded as another example of regression. Some of my patients remembered having had similar dreams in childhood, while in one case in which the terrifying image was a Chinaman, the dreamer distinctly recollected its occurrence in the dreams of his childhood. The images utilised in these examples of transformation were characteristic of an early period of life.

The examination of the nightmare and war-dream thus shows that they possess, though in a different way, a character which I have ascribed to dreams of the more ordinary kind. The nightmare and the war-dream share with dreams of other kinds the feature that they are occurrences in which experience finds expression in sleep in a form characteristic of infancy or of periods of life earlier than that of the occurrence of the dream. While it is not possible to regard all dreams either as wish-fulfilments or as successful solutions of conflicts, it is possible to bring them all into the category of regression, of throwing back in sleep to modes of mental activity and expression characteristic of earlier periods of life.

While the pure battle-dream thus differs from the general run of dreams in respect of transformation, it falls into line with the rest with regard to the infantile form in which the affect finds expression. The infantile character gives a broader basis for classification than is afforded by the process of transformation. This being so, let us inquire how far this infantile character is capable of explaining, or at least of illustrating, the relation of the affect to the dream.

I will begin with cases in which affect is absent. In my own " cup and saucer " dream the situation was ridiculous to anyone with the most elementary knowledge of billiards, and if there had been affect or affective expression corresponding with the manifest content of the dream, we should have expected it to have taken the form of amusement and laughter, both of which were certainly absent. If, however, the dream, as I have supposed, depended on the employment of a childish use of metaphor applied in a game with which the child was not familiar, there would be no special place for amusement or laughter. I acknowledge, however, that this dream is not well suited for the illustration of my point of view. For this purpose I shall use a dream which Freud has cited * in order to illustrate this topic. It is of a very unpleasant kind but peculiarly instructive for the light it throws on the problem before us. In this dream Freud cleansed the seat of a closet loaded with excrement by the same means as that adopted by Gulliver in order to put out the fire of the Lilliputian palace. In the dream Freud was wholly free from the disgust which such a scene would have aroused if it had been a real incident of his waking life, and he uses this dream to illustrate the absence of affect in the manifest dream when this is present in the deeper content. In a very interesting and instructive analysis of this dream Freud shows that it was the expression of a desire to be clear of unpleasant aspects of his professional work, and was a symbolic expression of a wish to clean out the Augean stables with which in a fit of despondency he tended to compare these surroundings. On the other hand, his own rôle as the Hercules of the occasion seemed to Freud to correspond with certain grandiose traits he detected in his own attitude towards the situation. Freud refers the absence of disgust in the dream to the fact revealed by his analysis that the thoughts of cleansing an Augean stable were combined with others of a pleasant kind referring to his own powers as a cleanser. The indifferent character of the dream in its affective aspect is referred to the combination of the two opposed kinds of affect present in the dream-thoughts.

On the view that the dream is an expression of infan-

* *Die Traumdeutung*, 5te Auflage, 1919, page 318; *The Interpretation of Dreams*, 1916, page 372.

tile modes of mental activity, another and a simpler
explanation of the absence of disgust becomes possible.
From this point of view Freud's dream is an expression
of a conflict between his desire to get away from certain
disgusting aspects of his professional work and the
desire for the beauties and pleasures of a holiday. The
dream produces a symbolic solution of the conflict by
getting rid of the disgusting aspects of his work by
means of a procedure which would make rect
appeal to the mind of a child and is in c nce
with a child's modes of activity. The a of
disgust in the dream seems to receive an ex on
more natural and at the same time more sir an
that given by Freud if in his dream he ha he
time regressed to an infantile attitude and wa ng
to purify his surroundings symbolically by a ire
characteristic of childhood. In the child su ro-
cedure would not arouse the emotion of dis nd
therefore no such emotion was aroused in th m.
The indifferent affective character of thi am
becomes natural and needs no elaborate ex ation
if the dream be an infantile mode of expression of a
wish-fulfilment or the solution of a conflict.

This dream of Freud's is one in which the absence
of affect in a situation where it might be expected
to occur is readily accounted for on the view that the
dream has an infantile character. Let us now turn
to examples of dreams accompanied by manifest
affect and inquire whether these also become explicable
on the view that the dream expresses infantile mentality. For this purpose let us turn to the dreams of
my patient.

The central situation of the suicide dream (see page
27) was one in which the dreamer was about to shoot
himself symbolically when he was stopped by the voice
of his son calling attention to the injury he would inflict
upon the boy if he carried out his design. There can be

no question that the homicidal situation presented by the dream would be at least as terrifying as, and probably far more terrifying, to the child than the suicide of which the dream-homicide was a symbolic expression. In this case the difference lies not so much in the relation between affect and the incident which called it forth, as in the nature of the affect itself. The infantile character shows itself in the intense and explosive, or as I have expressed it elsewhere,* in the " all-or-none " character of the affect, while in the real situation this would have had the more restrained form which emotion normally assumes in adult life.

Again, if the transference dream was an expression of infantile modes of feeling and acting, we have a case in which we may suppose that the child of the dream was being forced to turn away from one upon whom he had come to rely, and if current views concerning transference have any value, from one whom he had put in the position of his father. The intense affect of the dream, inappropriate perhaps to the actual situation of the dream, certainly inappropriate to the situation of having to turn from the help given to him by his physician, becomes wholly appropriate if in the dream the man had become again the child and was turning away from his father and ceasing to depend upon him for help and comfort.† The intensity of the affect becomes intelligible if the dream be a regression to infancy, just as the absence of affect becomes intelligible if the dream-situation is one which the infantile mind would regard with indifference.

I have so far dealt almost entirely with painful or unpleasant affect in its relation to the dream. It is now necessary to say something about the affects of a

* See *Instinct and the Unconscious*, page 117.
† I may point out here that the physical reaction of this dream has a clearly infantile character. The dreamer awoke vomiting, a mode of reaction to unpleasant situations far more frequent in infancy than in adult life.

. pleasant kind which so often accompany the dream. We have been led to connect the degree of intensity of painful affect present in the dream with the extent of the process of transformation, the absence of affect being correlated with the completeness of this process. I have supposed that the presence, nature and amount of affect present in the dream stand in no definite relation to the presence, nature and amount of affect accompanying the conflict to which the dream is due, but are determined by the attitude which would have been proper to the dreamer at the level of mental development active in the dream. If the level of mental activity which is active in the dream is that of childhood, and if the guise in which a conflict finds expression in a dream is one which would be terrifying to the child, the dream will be accompanied by affect in the form of terror. If, on the other hand, the imagery and symbolism in which a conflict is finding expression are of a kind so natural to the child that they would not be accompanied by affect, there will be no affect in the dream. The situation as portrayed in the dream may be one of adult life, but the dream-reaction is that of the child so far as affect is concerned.

If we now apply this point of view to the case in which the affect of a dream is of a pleasant kind, it will again be necessary to distinguish between dreams with varying degrees of transformation. We should expect pleasurable, as painful, affect to be the more definite, the less the degree of transformation. Where there is no transformation, we should expect the affective accompaniment to be considerable in amount. As an example of this may be cited the dreams of the kind, to which I have already referred incidentally, where the manifest content has a sexual nature. Here the pleasant nature of the affect is just as natural to the situation as the fear or terror accompanying a

79

dream of which the manifest content has reference to danger.

Another variety of dream accompanied by affect of a pleasant kind is that in which the manifest content has the nature of a day-dream. In this case again there is little if any transformation, but there is carried over into the dream an experience of waking life which in that waking life is definitely accompanied by pleasant affect. It may be suggested that the occurrence of the experience in sleep gives it that enhanced vividness and apparent reality which is characteristic of the day-dreams of childhood, and that the pleasantness of the affect is associated with this approach to an infantile character.

At the beginning of this chapter I mentioned a view of Freud to which I may now return for a moment. According to this writer, the lessening or disappearance of affect which accompanies the transformation of the latent into the manifest content of the dream is an effect ascribed to the censorship. As already mentioned, I have dealt elsewhere with the value of the concept of the censorship as a means of explaining or expressing the facts of transformation and disguise. I have referred these processes to the infantile character of the dream and have supposed that transformation and disguise are necessary consequences of this infantile character and would have occurred even if there had not been present the resistance for which Freud has adopted the simile of the censorship. It is evident that this point of view is equally applicable to the problem considered in this chapter. The absence of affect in Freud's "Augean stable dream," and its intense character in the dreams of the suicidal patient follow with equal readiness from the infantile character of the dream, and need no agency watching at the threshold of consciousness for their explanation. Freud's concept of the censorship was especially devised to meet the cases where affect is lessened or abolished and fails wholly to account for such dreams as those of my patient. The explanation of the nature of the affect in the dream as the necessary result of its infantile character not only renders the concept of the censorship unnecessary when it might seem to be appropriate, but it covers a wider field and is able to bring within its scope features of the dream with which this concept is wholly inadequate to deal.

I will conclude this chapter by stating the conclusions reached in it. I started from the position that dreams are attempts to solve in sleep conflicts of the waking life, and that these attempts are necessarily, from the nature of sleep, of a more or less infantile kind, since in sleep only the earlier levels of mental functioning are active. Next, I have supposed, and here I follow Freud, or at least agree with him, that the effect of transformation is to diminish or abolish the affective aspect of the conflict. Consequently, when there is no transformation, there is affect in the dream. This affect is painful when the conflict fails of solution, fails to satisfy the most prominent wishes of the dreamer. On the other hand, it is pleasant when these wishes are gratified. But in the majority of dreams the affective aspect is slight or absent because the struggle is transformed and the solution of the conflict only of a symbolic kind.

Moreover, just as I have argued that the transformation, ascribed by Freud to the need to evade the agency he calls the censorship, is a natural and indeed inevitable result of the expression of the conflict in the mental imagery and modes of mental functioning of early life, so do I now suppose that the affect has a similar infantile quality and that it is equally unnecessary to have recourse to the agency of the censorship to explain the relation between the manifest and latent contents of the dream so far as affect is concerned.

CHAPTER VI

" LONDON LECTURES " DREAMS

IN this chapter I propose to submit the record of a series of three dreams, occurring during one night, which illustrate several points of interest. They show, in the first place, the great importance which the manifest content may have as a guide to the deeper meaning of dreams. They illustrate, further, a point insisted on by Freud that all dreams occurring in one night can be referred to the same latent content ; and lastly, they will serve as an introduction to the problem why dreams are so easily forgotten and to the relation of the depth of sleep during which a dream is experienced to the nature of the dream.

The first dream began with a vague idea or image of having a sum of money in the form of large coins, either crowns or dollars. Then I was sitting at a table with the Master of my College who had a document before him which said that the Government was anxious to know of people who had money immediately available. He took down a record of the amount I possessed, which was very vague when I awoke, but the number 500 was more or less prominent. I awoke suffering from indigestion and began to think about the interpretation, when I fell asleep again and had a second dream, in which I was with a number of men who seemed to be lawyers. One of them read an essay, and then just as another, who was much like one of my patients, was about to read a second essay, he handed it to me to read for him. I was about to begin when I found that there was an introduction or abstract at the beginning, and I asked the chairman if I should read it. On his instructions I did so, and found a large number of difficult words over which I stumbled. Finally I came to two foreign words, one of which was something like ALMĪREẞ. I hesitated how to pronounce it, and especially how to give the second vowel, not being sure whether it should have the Italian or the ordinary English value. The writer of the essay called my attention to the fact that the correct pronunciation was given in a footnote. I had not seen this note and was still looking for it when I awoke. On thinking about this dream I was very surprised to find that I still remembered the previous dream. I intended to write them both down, but before I could do so, I went to sleep again. I had looked at my watch, in the meantime, however, and found that it was two o'clock.

I woke again about six o'clock with a third dream rather vaguely in my mind, in which there were two men who had apparently been rowing. They were talking about the second person plural, referring also to some other mode of expression which I supposed to be connected with rowing. The subject of the conversation was that this second expression had not been used on the occasion when they used the second person plural. Though the actual content of the dream was vague, it was clear to me that it dealt with a philological problem in which two linguistic peculiarities were associated, and the absence of one in the dream was accepted by me as a sufficient explanation of the absence of the other.

On awaking I was again surprised to find the two earlier dreams clearly in my mind, though I had not written them down. I could, however, see no meaning in the three dreams, nor could I get any clue to the manifest content. I then tried association with various elements of the dream without success, and was giving

83

up the task of analysis, when it flashed on me that on the preceding afternoon I had received a notice of lectures to be given in the following autumn at University College, London. I could not then remember what the lectures were about, but on getting up and recovering the notice from the waste-paper basket I was at once able to recognise several titles which had especially interested me when I read the list. These were :

THE ORIGINS OF COINAGE ;
PHONETICS AND ITS VALUE FROM THE IMPERIAL STANDPOINT ;
SCIENTIFIC METHODS OF LANGUAGE STUDY AND THEIR IMPORTANCE TO THE EMPIRE ; and
THE GROWTH OF COMPARATIVE LAW SINCE MAINE'S "ANCIENT LAW."

The first subject would account for the coins of the first dream and may have contributed to produce the strange words of the second dream. The two lectures on language would account for the general features of the second and third dreams, while the lecture on Comparative Law would not only account for the legal setting of the second dream, but would also help to explain the appearance of the Master of my College, for he is a lawyer. The manifest content of the three dreams was thus to a large extent explained by the items in the list of lectures which had especially attracted my attention on the preceding evening

The special interest of this dream, however, is that the explanation of its manifest content at once gave me the clue to its deeper meaning. At this time I was away from my hospital in Scotland on sick leave. A few days before I had heard that a project was on foot to give me an appointment in connection with the Royal Flying Corps, which would involve my living in London. When I read through the list of lectures, the thought had occurred to me that if the project went through, I might be able to attend some of these lectures and thus satisfy ethnological and sociological interests which were being starved in Edinburgh. The dreams thus appeared to be expressions of a rather simple wish to be given the new appointment. At the same time there was no question that the problem of this new appointment was the basis of a definite conflict in my mind. On the one side there was the desire for change and novelty, which is one of the strongest elements in my mental make-up, as well as the desire to become acquainted with the psychological and medical problems connected with flying. There was also the fact that I should be in much closer touch with my other interests in life, and one special factor was that I should be associated in the new investigations with Dr Head, in collaboration with whom so much of my work had been done. On the other side of the conflict were the facts that the new appointment would oblige me to leave my chief in Edinburgh, who was in a situation of peculiar difficulty, in which I knew that I might be of considerable service, and the change of work would also mean leaving to others the care of several patients in whom I was especially interested. On the evening before the dream I had written to one of these patients who was in a situation of a very difficult and complicated kind, in which I had some reason to believe that the outcome depended largely on my influence.

It was thus clear that the University College lecture-list which had evidently determined the general character of the manifest content of the three dreams had a definite relation to a conflict of a serious kind. In this conflict my own wishes were explicitly in favour of the new appointment, but these conflicted in the most direct manner with motives of an altruistic kind, involving duties and responsibilities towards

85

others. Dreams which at first sight seemed wholly inexplicable turned out to have a definite general relation to this conflict as soon as the explanation of the manifest content gave the necessary clue. It is not sufficient, however, or it should not be held to be sufficient, that a situation of the waking life should explain the general characters of a dream or dreams. It is also necessary to explain the details, and to these we may now turn.

The details of the first dream can be referred to a subsidiary conflict which was present at the time, and was one which would be affected by my change of post. I was at this time making an amply sufficient income for my needs through my pay as a Captain in the R.A.M.C., and I was at times worried by doubts whether I ought not to return to the College my income as Fellow, but I satisfied these doubts by investing every penny I could in war-loans, and the number 500 was certainly explained by the fact that this was the amount I had invested in this way. It thus became natural that the Master, as the natural representative or symbol, of my College, should have appeared in this dream.

The chief detail to be explained in the second dream was the appearance of the strange word which I found it difficult to pronounce. Association led me back at once to the early days of a visit to India, where I had been especially impressed for some reason by the fact that it is customary in that country to call a wardrobe an "Almeira." On the day before the dream I had been re-reading Charles Marriott's novel *The Column*, which was intimately associated with the early days of my visit to India and with the friend from whom I had first heard the word "Almeira" and learnt its meaning. The greater part of the strange word was thus intimately linked with the general philological setting of the three dreams, while its occurrence may also have been assisted by the announcement of a lecture on "Hindu Religion and Philosophy" in the University College list of lectures. The letter at the end of the word was certainly from the Greek alphabet, but though it resembled Xi in some respect, it was associated with the idea of Digamma. I failed wholly to explain this feature of the word.

The third dream contained two details which are very puzzling, while the whole character of the dream is obscure, apart from its general philological setting. I was quite unable to discover the meaning of the reference to the second person plural and was also much puzzled by the reference to rowing. One of the results of the move to London would be to allow me to visit Cambridge more often, and if the dream is an expression of youthful mentality, it is possible that rowing acted as a symbol for Cambridge, for in boyhood my chief interest in Cambridge had been through the boat race.

Though there are details of which the interpretation is lacking, there can be no question that the main features of the three dreams were determined by the conflict arising out of the prospect of a new appointment, the manifest content being determined by an incident of the previous day which had directly stimulated this conflict. I have cited this series of dreams primarily as an example of the way in which knowledge of the mode of determination of the manifest content may assist the discovery of the deeper meaning, but they have several other points of interest.

One such interest is the confirmation given by the dreams to the statement made by Freud that when several dreams occur to a person in one night they will all be found to refer to the same latent content. It is only very exceptionally that I have been able to analyse more than one dream occurring during a night, and it is noteworthy that on the sole occasion on which the analysis of three dreams should have been possible, all the three should be so clearly referable to one interpretation. It may be noted, however, that the connection of the third dream with the conflict about the appointment was less obvious than in the case of the two earlier dreams, and that the time-interval between this dream and its predecessors was probably longer than that between the first and second dreams.

I need hardly point out how natural it is that under ordinary circumstances all the dreams of one night should be referable to one latent content if the view put forward in these lectures is correct. Unless something should happen during the night which introduces a new cause of conflict, there ought to be no change in the nature of the deeper thoughts which are finding expression in the form of dreams. It is not necessary, however, that such dreams should have the high degree of unity which seems to be shown by those I have recorded. Thus, Abraham * mentions a case in which a woman had five dreams in one night which realised five different possibilities which might arise out of the situation in which she was placed at the time. In the language of this book the five dreams attempted five different solutions of the conflict in which she was involved.

A point of great interest of the dreams which I must now consider more fully is the ease, most unusual in my own case, with which the dreams were remembered. As a rule my dreams are forgotten very rapidly and have to be written down at once if a record is to become possible, but in this case I not only remembered the dreams more or less clearly when I awoke, but as much as was remembered when I awoke continued clearly in my mind after later sleep, the length of sleep before the third dream being as much as four

* *Dreams and Myths*, page 56.

hours. Combined with this was an impression, definitely recorded in my notes at the time, that I had been sleeping very lightly.

This experience raises the very important question why dreams are so readily forgotten. According to Freud this is one of the effects of the censorship. According to the hypothesis of the censorship, the occurrence of dreams depends upon relaxation of the activity of this agency watching at the threshold of consciousness, the activity being so far relaxed as to allow the buried dream-thoughts to appear in consciousness, though in distorted guise, and the forgetting is the natural result of the regained full activity of the censorship. An alternative view suggested by the dreams now under consideration is that whether dreams are remembered with ease or difficulty depends, at any rate partially, upon the depth of sleep, the dreams of light sleep being readily accessible, while those of deeper sleep are soon forgotten. This raises the question whether there is any relation between the depth of the sleep during which a dream is experienced and the character of the dream, and from this point of view the dreams I have just described are of interest. Except for the occurrence of imagery and the doubtful use of rowing as a symbol of Cambridge, these dreams can hardly be regarded as an example of infantile or even of youthful mentality. The imagery or symbolism in which the dream-thoughts were clothed was of an abstract and elaborate kind and only differed from the thought-processes of adult waking life in their inconsequent and erratic character.

Much other experience of my own dreams points in the same direction. Thus, I not infrequently have dreams in which I am reading a paper or giving a lecture which I am able to recall with ease when I awake, and I have always found when the content of a dream is thus easily remembered that it differs

89

very little, if at all, from what I might have written
or spoken if I had been in full waking activity. In
such a case it would be ridiculous to regard the dream
as an expression of infantile mentality, and experiences
of this kind have led me to the view that dreams
differ in character according to the depth of the sleep
during which they occur. The lighter the sleep which
a dream accompanies, the more nearly does it approach
in its character to the mode of mental functioning
proper to the age at which it occurs and the more
easily will the dream be remembered. This view
is a natural corollary of the scheme which I have put
forward elsewhere,* that the mind may be regarded
as composed of a number of levels or strata comparable with the levels of neurological activity which are
now widely held to furnish the best explanation of
the mode of action of the nervous system. According
to this view the deeper the sleep, the larger the number
of these levels which are put out of activity and the
lower the level which finds expression in the dream.
The dreams of deep sleep in which many levels of mental
activity are put out of action will reveal infantile
modes of thinking, feeling and acting ; the dreams of
less deep sleep in which fewer of the higher levels
are inactive would express modes of mental functioning
proper to childhood or youth ; while the dreams of
very light sleep would have a character but little
different from that of the ordinary mental activities
of the waking life.

The general point of view which I am developing
in this book was originally formulated in order to
account for the appearance of distortion or disguise
in the dream which forms Freud's chief argument for
the censorship. I now suggest that this view is also
able to account for the readiness with which dreams
are forgotten, a fact which Freud has also referred to

* *Instinct and the Unconscious*, 2nd Edition, 1922, page 229.

his mechanism of the censorship. Dreams, or rather certain dreams, are readily forgotten because they are the manifestations of levels of mental activity remote in character from those of later periods of life. According to the scheme put forward in my book *Instinct and the Unconscious*, early levels of mental activity are suppressed because they are incompatible with the activities of later life. The mental efficiency of a person would be greatly prejudiced if modes of thinking, feeling and acting proper to infancy or childhood were continually intruding into the activities of adult life, and from this point of view it is natural that when these early modes of mental functioning are brought into temporary activity during sleep, they should again pass into oblivion as rapidly as possible when the sleeper awakes.

One difficulty for this point of view must be considered here. There is one kind of dream of which memory is exceptionally vivid and, so far as can be told, accurate. One of the features of the nightmare is that it is not merely remembered on awaking, but it tends to persist with an unusual degree of vividness in the mind of the dreamer. Is this to be explained by the occurrence of this kind of dream in light sleep, or is it necessary to look for some other mode of explanation of the vivid memory of these dreams? I have little doubt that the answer is to be found in the second alternative and that we must look to the excess of affect which is characteristic of the nightmare and the battle-dream as furnishing the ground for the readiness and vividness with which their incidents persist in memory. It is probable, therefore, that depth of sleep is only one of the factors upon which persistence depends, and that in sleeping as in waking life there is a definite relation between the amount of affect associated with an experience and the persistence with which it is remembered. It must always be borne in mind in this connection that excess of affect may also be the cause, or one of the causes, of suppression or active forgetting. The importance of excess of affect in relation to memory is that it tends to be associated either with unusual persistence in memory or with more or less complete suppression. By excess of affect an experience may be prevented from occupying its place among the vast mass which is readily accessible to consciousness and only absent from it at any given moment because it is not the object of attention or has not been brought into the focus of attention by appropriate associations. But if an experience accompanied by excess of affect is not suppressed, it persists with a high degree of vividness, and I suggest that this vividness accounts for the ease and fidelity with which the incidents of a nightmare or battle-dream are remembered.

THE DREAM-PROCESSES AS REGRESSIVE

One of the chief general conclusions to which I have been leading in this book is that the character of the dream, and especially its apparently fantastic and grotesque features, are due to the fact that it is an expression of early modes of mental functioning which have been allowed to come into action, owing to the removal of higher restraining influences derived from the experience of later life.

I have supposed that sleep is a process which acts progressively upon successive levels of mental activity, first putting out of action the experience and modes of mental functioning which have been recently acquired. The deeper the sleep, the greater the number of such levels put out of action and the lower and earlier the levels which are left to manifest their special modes of activity in the dream. I suppose that in the process of waking the higher levels are successively released, beginning with the lower, the nature of a dream experienced during the process of waking being determined by the level which is manifesting its activity at the moment when the dream is experienced.

From this point of view the fantastic or grotesque nature of the dream is not due, as Freud supposes, to a process of distortion dependent on the necessity of eluding a guardian watching at the threshold of consciousness, but it is a necessary result of the infantile nature of the dream. I do not deny that the nature of the thoughts to which the dream is due are disguised from the dreamer, and it is possible, if not probable, that this disguise has a useful function, but even if there were no such utility, the dream would have this fantastic character which is a necessary consequence of its regressive origin.

According to this point of view, a dream appears the more fantastic or grotesque to the dreamer when awake, the deeper the level of mental functioning upon which the dream depends. The deeper the level the more strange and unlike his normal self will the dream and the dream-personality seem to be. Moreover, it will follow that the more a person has changed in his modes of mental functioning during his life, the greater will be the difference between his dreams and the processes of his normal adult life, the greater also the difference between the dream-personality and the personality of the ordinary waking life.

One interest of this point of view is that it serves to explain a feature of the dream about the existence of which there seems to be little doubt, viz., that there is a relation between the complexity and amount of transformation of the dream and the degree of education of the dreamer. My experience of the dreams of uneducated persons is that they are exceedingly simple and their meaning often transparent,

93

as in the example I cited in the first lecture, and I believe that this is in accordance with general experience. It is the result of education, and I may say that I am not here limiting this term to the formal process of school and university. Education widens interest and produces a continuous process of modification in the mental make-up. The characteristic of the uneducated person is that the mental outlook of adult life does not differ appreciably from that of childhood, while the mind of the person who continues his education throughout life is that the whole mental make-up of mature adult life may be vastly different from that of his childhood or his youth or even of his younger adult life. To give an instance in illustration: In some of us older people the educative influence of the last ten years has been so great that we should hardly recognise ourselves if we were brought face to face. I suggest that the dream is a process whereby we are thus brought face to face with these earlier selves Speaking for myself, I am quite prepared to believe that if I had a dream in just that depth of sleep which found expression in the thoughts and sentiments of ten years ago, the dream has to some extent that strange and fantastic character which I ascribe to its regressive nature.

There is little doubt that I have been led to stress the importance of the point of view according to which the dream is a regression to a special feature of my own mental make-up which creates a striking difference between my dream-personality and the personality of my ordinary life. In my dreams I am a visualiser; I also often have perfectly definite auditory imagery, and less frequently imagery of other kinds, such as of taste and smell. In my ordinary life, on the other hand, I rarely experience imagery, and then usually in so fugitive and vague a form that if my attention had not been attracted to the subject through my scientific interests, I should doubtless never have noticed such capacity for imagery as I possess.

Moreover, as I have described elsewhere,* I know that in early life the power of imaging was present, and was probably as good as that of the average child. I have brought forward evidence to show that the disappearance of the capacity to image was the result of a process of suppression, which probably began before the age of five and has since become more complete.

If this history of my capacity to image be accepted, it will follow that when I image in my dreams, my dream-consciousness is utilising an infantile process which is not at my disposal in my ordinary waking life. The action of sleep in my case is to remove the activity of certain restraining or suppressing influences, whereby the power of imagery is kept in abeyance, but the reappearance of the power to image in sleep shows that it is there in my mental make-up, only waiting to come into action when the removal of the restraining influences gives it freedom. The view which I am now putting forward is that just as my power of imaging is normally suppressed and only finds expression in sleep, so is it with other early modes of mental functioning. Thus, all that I know of myself goes to convince me that in my adult waking life it is quite foreign to me to think in terms of the symbols of an incongruous person in surroundings to which he is unsuited by such a simile or metaphor as that of a cup and saucer as an element in a game of billiards. Nor in my dreams can I remember that I ever thought in such similes, but my experience in regard to imagery leads me to suspect that I was once subject to such ways of thinking, and that the use of such similes in a dream is only another expression of an early mode of mental functioning.

* *Instinct and the Unconscious,* page 11.

95

CHAPTER VII

THE CONTENT OF DREAMS

IT has so far been my object to consider the processes or, as they are sometimes called, the mechanisms of the dream, the processes by which mental conflicts, wishes, anxieties or other states find expression in sleep. I have described and given examples of such processes as symbolisation, dramatisation and condensation through which these mental states receive concrete representation in the dream. I have tried to find how far we are justified in accepting a process of displacement as a fourth element in the dream-work, and have considered how far we can ascribe to this and the other elements of the dream-work the function of disguise and distortion in the interests of the continuance of sleep. The conclusion to which I have been led is that the special character of the dream is not due, as Freud supposes, to the activity of a process of censorship leading to a distortion of the real meaning of the dream, so that this meaning shall not be recognised by the dreamer, but is the result of the fact that the dream depends on the coming into activity in sleep of early modes of mental functioning. I have regarded the symbolisation and dramatisation of the dream as processes characteristic of childhood and youth, which come into activity in sleep, because more recent modes of mental functioning have passed into abeyance in sleep, with the consequent removal of the control which in the waking life they normally exert on older activities. From this point of view the dream may be regarded as a regressive state, including under the word all the earlier phases of mental development.

When the dream is regarded as regressive or infantile, however, something very different from this is often meant. When we speak of the dream as an expression of infantile mentality, this may mean two very different things. It may refer to the infantile character of the processes of the dream or it may mean that the dream has an infantile content. Thus far it is only in the first of these two senses that I have dealt with the regressive character of the dream ; it remains to consider how far the content of the dream is derived from the experience of earlier life.

It has been a striking feature of all the dreams related and analysed in this book that they have been concerned with recent conflicts. Their latent content has not been derived from the early experience of the dreamer, but has dealt with conflicts active in the mind of the dreamer at the time that the dream occurred.

Most of the analyses of dreams which we owe to the psycho-analytic school, on the other hand, take us back to conflicts or wishes forming the latent content which are frequently, if not generally, derived from the experiences of early life. It is necessary to deal with this discrepancy between the two sets of results. The first point to note is that the vast majority of dreams recorded in psycho-analytic literature, and utilised in support of psycho-analytic beliefs, have occurred in the course of treatment in which the attention of the dreamer has been led back to the experience of early life. Conflicts dating back to some early period of life have been revived and brought into great prominence in the waking consciousness of the dreamer. I have myself recorded dreams occurring in the course of psycho-therapy which well illustrate this point. Thus, the patient with claustrophobia, whose case I have recorded in Appendix II of *Instinct and the Unconscious*, had several dreams, the content of which dated back to the period of life which we were then trying to explore.

If, on the other hand, we turn to such a record of dreams and their analysis as that given by Freud himself in the *Traumdeutung*, we find a striking similarity with those which I have analysed with respect to the recency of the conflicts they reveal, a considerable proportion referring to situations arising out of Freud's professional career closely comparable with those which have provided the motives of so many of my own dreams. Moreover, in Freud's discussion of the varieties of source upon which dreams depend, the conclusions which emerge agree with those I have just stated. If objection is made to my record of dreams on the ground of the recency of the conflicts upon which they depend, we have only to go to Freud * for confirmation, excepting only those cases which must be regarded as of a more or less artificial kind, in which dreams occur as incidents in the course of a psychoanalysis.

Though dreams going back to early experience as their source frequently occur under such circumstances, it is far from necessary that the dreams of patients under treatment shall have this character. Thus, the patient's dreams recorded in Chapter II had as their source a conflict of quite recent origin which was raging at the time that the dream occurred. I will now cite another dream of a patient which also had recent conflict as its source.

THE " ICHTHYOSAURUS " DREAM

In this dream the patient was being accused of the murder of two people in Paddington Station, while an ichthyosaurus was looking on. While being taken

* *Die Traumdeutung*, 5te Auflage, 1919, pages 125-6.

away by the police, the ichthyosaurus spat venom at him. The dreamer was taken to a Court of Justice where a letter was produced which incriminated him, but made no mention of his brother who had also been concerned in the murder. The dreamer awoke frightened and sweating.

The dream was probably an example of a war-dream in which the war experience had been completely transformed, for the dreamer was still liable occasionally to dreams of the nightmare kind, of which the content was actual war experience. I need not go into the explanation of the manifest content, the origin of which we were able to trace. The consideration of the dream led back at once to events of the previous day. The patient was an active member of a Committee which was concerned with the regulation of games, supply of writing materials and other matters managed by the patients. On the previous day he had found that certain changes were being made in the hospital which involved the temporary loss of the use of a writing-room, and, in common with another member of the Committee, he believed that this was being done by the matron and assistant matron with the connivance of the steward and behind the back of the C.O. of the hospital. The dreamer was a business man who had served through several years of the war. While on active service he had always been especially concerned for the comfort of his men. and in this connection had repeatedly come into conflict with battalion quartermasters, so that he had developed what would sometimes be called a "quartermaster complex," or, as I should prefer to call it, an anti-quartermaster sentiment, which helped to make him suspicious of the steward of the hospital, who was virtually its quartermaster. It seemed clear that the steward was represented in the dream by the ichthyosaurus, and that the two people of whose murder he was being accused were the matron and the assistant matron, while his brother seemed to have stood in the dream for the other patient with whom he had been associated in the matter of the writing-room. I cite this as an example of a dream which had a recent experience as its source, occurring in a patient under treatment, and one in which the experience was not connected, or only very remotely connected, with his illness. The dream arose out of a situation which might just as well have arisen in any other relation. It had as its source a quite recent experience, and in this respect falls into line with the other dreams which I have utilised in this book.

The anti-quartermaster sentiment of this patient was well illustrated a few days later by another dream about a similar situation in which the disguise was less complete. In this dream he received orders to obtain rations before marching with his company. He was in one of the narrow streets paved with cobbles near the Cathedral in Rouen, and went to the quartermaster-general's stores, where he found nothing left but pieces of smoked salmon hanging from the rafters. After much discussion, in which the dreamer laid great stress on his indifference to the exact amount, so long as the distribution was equal, he went off with two pieces of the salmon. His men groused badly, and he told them it did not matter how little they had, so long as they got their proper share. He said that they had not been able to get their proper amount this time, because the quartermaster had favoured other company-commanders, and that he would see that they had their proper share in future.

This dream occurred at a time when the food in the hospital was very inadequate. The patient would not have minded if he had known that this was due to the necessity for national economy or to the insufficiencies of the kitchen staff, but he could not help the conviction that the person who was reaping the advantage was the steward. I might mention that one of the functions of the Committee, of which the patient was a prominent member, was to bring any complaints before the officer commanding the hospital, so that he had a real cause for anxiety and conflict in the matter. At the time that these dreams occurred, nothing was being done to bring the early life of the dreamer into the focus of attention or to arouse early conflicts. The dreams thus confirm the conclusions reached by myself and implied in Freud's own classification of the sources of the dream. Unless some process is taking place which tends to arouse early experience and bring it into prominence, dreams deal with situations in the recent life of the dreamer.

The view generally held by the psycho-analytic school, and widely accepted by others, that the content of dreams is so frequently experience derived from early life does not, however, rest solely on the frequency of early experience as the motive of dreams taking place in the course of psycho-analysis. The typical dreams of Freud are believed also to point in this direction. Thus, the dreams of nakedness or scanty clothing experienced by so many persons are ascribed to impulses of exhibition which are common in childhood, and the equally frequent dreams of the death of dearly loved persons are led back to the frequent wishes of children, ill acquainted with the implications of death, that their parents or other relatives should die.

It is a feature of most dreams of this kind that they are recurrent and occur again and again, sometimes in precisely similar form, and when they have this recurrent character, it is probable that they go back, at any rate in some measure, to early experience. I shall return to this topic when considering typical and recurrent dreams in a later chapter, and shall only deal here with dreams of this kind when they occur sporadically, choosing for illustration the dreams that dearly loved persons are dead.

Such dreams have naturally formed an obstacle to the acceptance of Freud's view that every dream is a wish-fulfilment, an obstacle which has been partly overcome by the reference of many of these dreams to the recurrence of early wishes of childhood. Freud has also shown, however, that wishes for the death of dearly loved relatives may occur in adult life and act as the motive of dreams. In one well-known and striking example * he records a dream of this kind, in which the desire for the death of a nephew is interpreted as the result of a wish to meet an old lover, a meeting which would naturally take place at the funeral of the nephew who died in the dream. When the thought that if the nephew died the lover would come to the funeral came to mind, we must suppose that it was at once repressed, but that the conflict so aroused only remained below the threshold, to become again active in sleep, owing to the absence of restraining influences derived from adult modes of thought, the wish for the death of the nephew being then given full rein. The dream agrees exactly with the view that in the dream infantile modes of thought come into activity, though the actual motive of the dream was a quite recent wish for an opportunity of a much desired meeting. I have met with several cases in which dreams that relatives were dead, or had suffered misfortunes, have been explained in a similar, though perhaps rather simpler fashion, and I will relate two examples.

DREAMS ARISING OUT OF RECENT EVENTS

One of my patients came to me much distressed because in a dream of the previous night he had shot a

* *Traumdeutung*, 5te Auflage, page 107 : *Interpretation of Dreams*, page 128.

younger brother of whom he was especially fond. The dreamer had had a very trying time in France, under the strain of which he had broken down. The brother whom he had murdered in the dream was being trained for active service, and it transpired that the dreamer was so greatly worried about his brother and the trials awaiting him in France, that he had allowed himself to think it better that the brother were dead rather than that he should be exposed to such experiences as those he had himself undergone. This wish for the death of the brother was naturally repressed in the waking state, but found expression through the act of a dream, when sleep had removed the activity of the restraining influences derived from the social attitude of our society towards wishes for the death either of others or ourselves.

Another patient, whose wife was shortly expecting a child, had several dreams by which he was much disturbed. In one he visited his wife in a nursing home, and she upbraided him severely for her pregnancy. She said she did not wish to have a child, and told her husband that she wished never to see him again. On another occasion he dreamed that his child had been born and that it was a kind of cross between a rabbit and a monkey, but that his wife was so delighted with the child that she ran about clapping her hands.

In reality his wife was very pleased at the prospect of becoming a mother and was showing no anxiety about her approaching ordeal, but the patient was greatly worried about his financial position. More than once he had found himself wishing that he were not about to have a child in his present circumstances, but these wishes had been at once repressed.

The aim of this chapter has been to show not only by means of facts collected by myself, but also through the evidence of Freud himself, how frequently dreams arise out of situations in the recent life of the dreamer.

THE CONTENT OF DREAMS

Excepting the case of recurrent dreams, it is probable that dreams always arise out of recent situations, unless something has taken place which has aroused ancient conflicts and brought them again into prominence in the mind of the dreamer. The special aim of the process of psycho-analysis is to bring the experience of early life into such prominence, and it is therefore natural that this procedure should have obscured the importance of recent conflicts. It is intelligible that those whose experience is chiefly derived from the psycho-analytic study of the dreams of their patients should have laid so great a stress on the importance of infantile experience as the source of the dream-content.

COMPARISON WITH FREUD'S VIEWS

The close agreement between most of the dream-analyses of Freud and my own, in so far as concerns the recency of the conflicts upon which dreams depend, raises the question why there should be so widespread a belief among psycho-analysts that the source of dreams is to be found in wishes of early childhood.

One reason, and probably the most important, is that while Freud used comparatively few dreams of his patients when formulating his scheme of dream-formation, the general body of psycho-analysts rely mainly on such dreams for their evidence, and when they utilise their own dreams are influenced by the use of a method of analysis by free association, which they have come to associate with early experience, so that such experience tends especially to occur to their minds. The only passage which I have been able to find which seems to express Freud's own attitude towards the problem raised by the discrepancy between his own evidence and the view concerning the importance of early experience is one in which he regards a conflict between vanity and self-criticism as having determined the content of a dream, but supposes that it was only a more deeply seated wish of youth which had made this content possible as a dream.*

The idea which seems to underlie this opinion is that a recent conflict will not find expression in a dream unless a wish of early life is also active. So far as I can gather from other writings of Freud, it is held that the function of this early wish is to supply the energy or drive necessary for the appearance of the dream, but I cannot say definitely that this is so. My view is that conflict is quite sufficient.

This seems a suitable place to consider a theoretical difficulty which stands in the way of the view I am putting forward in this book, one which might possibly be met by some such view as that expressed by Freud in the passage I have quoted. If the special character of dreams depend on putting out of action the levels or more recently acquired experience, how does it come about that recent conflicts, which must be included in the levels of recently acquired experience, should be so active in the dream, and that recent experience should also supply the motives for the details of the manifest content ? If my general position is to hold good, it becomes necessary to discover how it is that a conflict which forms part of quite recent experience should provide the essential motive for a dream, when the expression of this conflict by means of infantile symbolism suggests that it is early modes of mental functioning which are mainly or even wholly in action. My hypothesis is here met by a very serious and it might be thought insuperable difficulty. Before considering it, let us state clearly the chief factors entering into the problem. We have found that dreams are the expression of recent conflicts, a conclusion

* *Traumdeutung*, 5te Auflage, page 324 (Brill's translation, page 379).

confirmed by Freud himself, at any rate in so far as the determination of the content of the dream is concerned, and that by universal consent the manifest content is determined by recent experience. Next we have found that most dreams consist of imagery, symbols, similes, etc., which, at any rate in some cases, do not form part of the mental furniture óf the adult life of the dreamer but belong to earlier periods of his life, this being especially striking in such a person as myself, from whose adult mental life images have almost completely disappeared for many years. In order to explain the second fact, I have hitherto been content to adopt the hypothesis that the conflict finds expression in this form because the infantile modes of mental functioning are alone available when the higher or more recently acquired modes of mental functioning have been put out of activity in sleep. We now have to deal with the difficulty that according to the hypothesis in this crude form the recent conflicts which find expression in the dream, as well as the experience determining the manifest content, being part of recent experience, should have been put out of activity, so that they could not function in the way supposed. It is evident that the proposition that in sleep different levels of experience are put out of action successively in chronological order is only a crude statement of the case, and that this part of the hypothesis needs more exact expression. The solution of the problem evidently lies in a more exact statement of the nature of sleep, and to this subject we must therefore turn.

In my chapter on sleep in *Instinct and the Unconscious* I have considered at some length the power of selective attention which is possible in sleep. There are many facts which demand the existence of a high degree of discriminative activity on the part of a sleeping person in relation to certain kinds of external stimuli.

THE CONTENT OF DREAMS

In the chapter cited I quote especially the awakening of the doctor by his night bell while he is not disturbed by the crying of his infant to which his wife immediately responds. Such facts make it evident that sleep is not a process which puts out of action different levels of mental activity and mental experience in chronological order, but that certain parts of recent experience remain active even in deep sleep.

In my book I have regarded the conditions which awake a person as determined by special systems within the personality of the sleeper, and it is not difficult to see how this view can be extended, so as to explain the activity of a recent conflict in sleep. We must regard this conflict as being, or forming part of, a special system within the personality of the sleeper, which still remains active after the process of sleep has put out of action other recent experience and modes of mental functioning.

We must suppose that when experience is the subject of a mental conflict, or is more or less intimately associated with such a conflict, it fails to undergo the process of suppression which is one of the chief elements of the process of sleep, but remains active, ready to find expression in a dream. Two subsidiary difficulties attendant on this point of view have to be met. The first is that in order to explain the occurrence of incidents from recent experience as elements of the manifest content, we have to suppose that these incidents are not trivial and indifferent, but are in some way connected with the conflict, so that they form part of the system which remains active after other recent experience has been inhibited in the process of sleep. I have already dealt with this topic and have shown reason to believe that the incidents determining the manifest content have not the trivial character ordinarily supposed, but can often be shown to stand in an intimate relation to the subject-matter of the conflict which is finding expression in the dream. We need far more observations on this point. There is a tendency at present unduly to neglect the manifest content, probably as a reaction against the exclusive interest of so many of the older students in this aspect of the dream. But if we are to understand the dream, we cannot neglect any of its aspects, and the theoretical position now put forward requires a careful inquiry into the exact nature of the relation between the incidents which have determined the manifest content and the conflict which forms the latent content of the dream.

The second difficulty is that if certain elements of recent experience remain active in sleep, we should expect these elements to influence the general character of the dream. We should expect that the dream in general would not show an exclusively regressive form of mentality, but that there would be features of the dream which would reveal a mentality resembling that of the period of life at which the dream is experienced. I would meet this difficulty by saying that, as a matter of fact, the dream shows just such variety as we might expect to follow from the retention of activity of certain kinds of recent experience. Thus, to take only one instance, while the suicide dream recorded in Chapter II shows on the whole an infantile mentality, the representation of suicide by the image of Dr X, who had himself recently committed suicide, was just such an example as would be utilised by the adult, and had actually influenced the thoughts of the dreamer. Moreover, it is significant that this representation, derived from recent experience, which was prominent in the dream, was intimately connected with the conflict which was the chief source of the dream. If certain streaks, as it were, of recent experience remain active after the greater part of this recent experience has been put out of action in sleep, many features of the variegated character of the dream become explicable, which wholly fail to fit in with the simple view that the higher levels of mental activity are wholly inhibited in sleep.

When, therefore, I speak of the dream as an expression of regressive mentality, this must only be taken to apply to the general character of the dream, and that the non-infantile features which are often present are due to the persistent activity of such elements of experience as are closely bound up with the conflict which forms the active source of the dream. The system which is active in the dream comprises two parts. One consists of such levels of early activity as still remain in action with the depth of sleep which is present ; the other of such portions of the total body of recent experience which, on account of the connection with a conflict and consequent recent excitation, still continue active after the rest of the levels embodying recent experience have been put out of action by the inhibition of sleep.

In considering the nature of the dream-content I have so far dealt only with its time-aspect, with the question how far the conflicts determining dreams are derived from recent experience and how far they date back to earlier periods of life. The general tendency of my argument has been to emphasise the importance of recent conflicts and to assume that, when early conflicts form the sources of the dreams, this is because they have been revived in waking life and again brought into prominence, the most frequent instances of this revival at the present time arising out of activity of the psycho-analysts.

Time, however, forms only one aspect of the topic of dream-content, and this seems to be a convenient moment to consider briefly the nature of the experience involved in the conflicts upon which dreams depend. I am the first to recognise that my own material is of a special kind. It is derived from two sources: one, the dreams of soldiers suffering from the effects of war experience, with active conflicts arising out of this experience; the other, my own dreams, where sexual conflicts might perhaps hardly be expected to be as active as in the dreams of younger people. Moreover, most of my own dreams which have been analysed occurred at a time when, owing to the extreme interest of my work and my absorption in it, I was far more free than usual from the sexual conflicts which are generally believed to be active in dreams. Many of the dreams which I analysed at this time could be referred to conflicts connected with my work, while another very interesting series, of which I have not yet given you an example, seemed to be explained by certain conflicts arising out of my attitude towards the war. So far as my positive evidence goes, sexual conflicts find expression in my own dreams with relatively little transformation and disguise, and it is only rarely that I have been able to explain a dream devoid of manifest sexual aspects as a conflict of a sexual kind. It is quite possible, of course, that when such conflicts are in action, there is an unusually great resistance, and that this resistance accounts for my not infrequent complete failure to analyse a dream. But even if this be the case, it must be remembered that the conditions under which my own dreams occurred were in many ways exceptional, and that sexual conflicts, transformed so as to be unrecognisable at first sight, would almost certainly be far more frequently active in a younger person and one less absorbed in special forms of mental activity. Because my own dreams can be referred comparatively rarely to conflicts of a sexual kind, it must not be concluded that sexual conflicts are not frequent, probably even the most frequent, sources of dreams. I am inclined to believe that it is just because the dreams I have analysed happen to be so largely independent of sex that they furnish examples especially suited for the purpose of demonstration. If they had dealt with sex-conflicts the analyses would probably have been full of passages which a natural reticence would have driven me to withhold or garble, thus interfering with the cogency of the demonstration. Moreover, in addition to such witting and clearly recognised obstructions, there would probably have been also others of an unwitting kind dependent on the resistance for which Freud has adopted the, in my opinion, unsuitable simile of the censorship. It is, I think, natural that this resistance should show less activity in the case of such comparatively innocent conflicts as those to which I have referred my dreams than might be expected if the conflicts had been concerned with sex.

DISPLACEMENT

On several occasions in this book I have referred to difficulties connected with the process of displacement which, according to Freud, forms a prominent element of the dream-work, and is one of the chief agencies, if not the chief agency, in disguising from the dreamer the real nature of the thoughts to which his dreams are due. If by displacement we only mean the process by which elements of the latent content find expression in a symbolic or other form, which prevents the recognition of their true nature by the dreamer, the dreams which have been recorded and analysed in this book afford numerous instances of its occurrence, but it is clear that Freud means something more than this. According to him displacement is a process in which the interest attaching to a prominent element of the latent content is not transferred to the element or elements of the manifest content by means of which it is symbolised, but is displaced so as to become attached to some other insignificant image of the dream. The image which is most prominent in the manifest dream is not regarded as a symbol of the leading wish or other element to which the dream is due, but is an image of an indifferent kind to which the prominence has been displaced.

Displacement of this kind occupies a very prominent position in Freud's scheme, because to this process is especially ascribed the distortion which the latent content of a dream is believed to undergo in order that it may elude the vigilance of the censorship. There is little question that it is the weight laid by Freud on the necessity for distortion and disguise which has led him to take so great an interest in, and attach so much importance to, this process.

In the dreams of my own and of other persons which I have analysed I have been unable to confirm the presence of displacement in this sense. Thus, in my own "Presidency" dream the prominent element in the latent content was certainly the wish to be President with the conflict connected with this wish, and the prominent element in the manifest dream was with equal certainty the occurrence of the name of " S. Poole," who had been nominated as President by the dream-consciousness. In the suicide dream of my patient the prominent element of the deeper content was undoubtedly the impulse to suicide, and few would hesitate to accept the incident in which the dreamer took up the revolver to shoot his dream-surrogate as the outstanding feature of the manifest dream. In my own " cup and saucer " dream the outstanding feature of the latent content was the disturbing patient, for with him were connected the egoistic elements which really determined that the rearrangement of rooms should become the subject of a dream, and the cup and saucer by which he was symbolised in the dream formed the outstanding feature of the manifest content. In the three dreams which expressed my wish to go to London, the matter is less simple, but the prominent objects in all three manifest dreams were directly connected with the lectures, the information about which had acted as the immediate means of strengthening this wish.

My own evidence having thus failed to confirm one of the most important parts of Freud's scheme of the process by which wishes or other forms of mental content find expression in the dream, let us turn to Freud's own record and inquire into the nature of the dream and dream-analyses upon which he has founded his conclusions. I will begin with the dream of the botanical monograph with which Freud starts his consideration of displacement.* This dream is very short, so that it can be given in full :

" I have written a monograph upon a certain plant. The book lies before me, I am just turning over a folded coloured plate. A dried specimen of the plant is bound with every copy, as though from a herbarium."

After considering certain incidents which had determined the manifest content, Freud was led by the process of free association to the complications and conflicts that result from services rendered among colleagues, which put them under obligations to one another, and from these he was led to the reproach that he was accustomed to sacrifice too much to his hobbies. He regards " botanical " as the central point of the manifest dream,† and finds no place for this element in the nucleus of his dream-thoughts.

Only one such connection could be found, viz., that as botany was not one of his favourite studies,

---

* *Traumdeutung*, 5te Auflage, page 118 (Brill's translation, page 142).
† *Ibid.*, page 209 (Brill's translation, page 284).

there would have been an antithetical relation between the central point of his dream-thoughts and the element "botanical," which he regards as the outstanding feature of the manifest dream.

Let us now examine the dream and its associations for ourselves. The first point to be noted is the prominent place taken in the associations by the fact that Freud had once himself written a botanical essay (Aufsatz). Moreover, this essay on the coca plant had called the attention of K. Koller to its anæsthetic properties, and Freud himself clearly recognised in his analysis that, if he had been more thorough, he might himself have made the discovery which Koller made as the result of reading Freud's essay. It is evident that this early essay of Freud was of very great importance, and if, instead of picking out "botanical" as the central point of the manifest dream, Freud had regarded "botanical essay " as this central point, this nucleus would have been closely connected with an incident of Freud's life of great importance. One cannot help suspecting that the reproaches concerning hobbies which were reached in Freud's analysis were not altogether disconnected with his failure to discover the possibilities connected with the anæsthetic properties of cocaine.

Let us now turn again to Freud's analysis. In the evening before the dream Freud had had a long conversation with Dr Koenigstein, an eye-specialist, in which subjects were considered which touched Freud closely and awakened memories revealing the most diverse feelings of his inner self. We are told that among the subjects touched on in this conversation were cocaine and Freud's preference for monographic studies. But had it also included, or even touched, such a topic as Freud's position in the world as a psychiatrist, there would have been another definite connection with the essay on *coca*, for if this work had led Freud to discover the practical value of cocaine as an anæsthetic, it would have had an enormous influence upon his career. If he had been known to the world as the discoverer of cocaine his psychological doctrines would have had far greater chances of acceptance. Even if the conversation with the eye-specialist did not directly touch this aspect of Freud's life, the mere fact that his friend was an eye-specialist would have been enough, for there is no branch of medical practice in which cocaine is more important than in ophthalmology.

After considering his conversation with Dr Koenigstein Freud sums up the analysis by assigning to the dream the meaning. " I am the man who has written that valuable and successful treatise (Abhandlung) on cocaine." One cannot help suspecting that a process by which the word " Abhandlung " (treatise) was substituted for "Aufsatz" (essay), when Freud was writing, was responsible for obscuring the meaning ; and that if this substitution had not taken place, Freud might have been quicker to recognise that " botanical essay" rather than "botanical" was really the central point of the manifest content.

I have not finished. Freud was not able to analyse this dream until the evening of the day following the dream, but during the morning of this day he had a kind of day-phantasy. According to my point of view such a phantasy is far more likely to lead to the essential content of the dream than the method of free association, which (especially after the interval of a whole day's experience) is likely to introduce a number of irrelevant topics. It is therefore of great interest that this day-phantasy dealt explicitly with cocaine and with the share which Freud had had in its discovery.

I suggest, therefore, that the very first dream cited by Freud as an example of a process of displacement of the deeper meaning to an unessential element of the manifest content not only fails to confirm his conclusion, but provides definite evidence (so far as it is possible to obtain such evidence from the re-examination of a published analysis), that there was no such displacement.

In this re-examination of Freud's analysis the only new factor which I have introduced is the great effect which his fame as the discoverer of cocaine would have had on the acceptance of Freud's psychological doctrines, which is by no means essential to the analysis. In every other part of my re-examination I have only slightly altered the stress laid on facts definitely recorded by Freud himself, and by this alteration of relative stress have brought out the fact that underlying the image of a botanical monograph, which was the central feature of the manifest dream, there lay a system of reproaches and regrets arising out of a botanical essay written by Freud in early life.

CHAPTER VIII

THE " REPROACHFUL LETTER " DREAM

In the history of my attitude towards Freud's theory
of the dream, which I gave in the first chapter, I related
how a sceptical tendency was overcome by the experience of a dream arising out of a latent desire to be
President of a Society. One result of this dream was
to make me a temporary convert to the view that the
dream expresses the fulfilment of a wish. It was not
long, however, before I had other dreams which fitted
less easily with this formula, and I was led by them
to the view that instead of the dream being always
the fulfilment of a wish, it might be the expression
of any other affective state. At this time it seemed
to me probable that dreams were so often the expression of desire, because desire is so frequent and so
prominent among our affective states. Other experiences, and especially the occurrence of dreams referable
to anxiety, which not only came into my own experience
but were still more prominent in the minds of my
patients, led me to the view that dreams might be
the expression of any affective state of which the
dreamer had been the subject during the preceding
day.

During the time when this view was forming in my
mind I had a dream which seemed at first sight to
give it striking confirmation. I propose to devote
the greater part of this chapter to a consideration
of an unusually complicated analysis of which this
dream has been the subject.

THE " REPROACHFUL LETTER " DREAM

The earliest feature of this dream, which occurred at Craiglockhart about 2.15 A.M. during the night of 20th–21st March 1917, that I could recall is that I was reading a letter from a Cambridge friend. On waking I could not remember the details of the letter, but its general purport was to reproach me for my political views. In accordance with the real habit of the writer, the letter was in an allusive style, only referring indirectly to the grounds for his displeasure, but these grounds seemed quite obvious to me in the dream, and the highly reproachful character of the communication was evident. I did not reach the end of the letter and was not aware on waking that I had seen the signature, though I had no doubt about the identity of the writer. I passed insensibly from reading the letter to the consideration of its subject-matter. The political views with which my friend was reproaching me were connected with the general European situation at the time. The thoughts to which I passed from the reading of the letter dealt particularly with the theme that the misfortunes of the Entente powers had been due to lack of co-ordination among its members. One of these thoughts which stood out especially clearly in my mind when I had become definitely awake was that the lack of co-ordination among the members of our own Government, which had come to light a short time before in the Dardanelles Report, would certainly have been present in even greater degree when the co-ordination needed had to be between the rulers of different countries. About this phase of the experience there came to my mind the list of the new French Ministry which had appeared in the paper the day preceding the dream. I saw this list clearly in just the visual form in which it had

118

appeared in the newspaper. I believe that I saw the whole list in the paper of the dream, but on waking I could only remember the names of Ribot, Viviani and Thomas, and the absence of the name of Briand. The sight of this list started a line of speculation concerning the reasons for the change of Ministry. I wondered how far it indicated a diminution in the strength of the *jusqu' au boutiste* element in France, and proceeded to think about the possible influence of the change on the conduct of the war.

About this point I became aware that I was awake and that I had had a dream. I wrote down at once all that I could remember.

On proceeding to the analysis it was obvious that the experience was a characteristic example of the process which I have described in Chapter I, in which the dream proper had passed insensibly into thoughts of the half-waking state. The experience resembled exactly that which, as I have stated, has produced so much of my scientific work, with the difference that the subject-matter of the half-waking thoughts was the political situation of the moment instead of the scientific problems which usually form the object of such thoughts. There was no clear dividing line between the reading of the letter with which the dream began and the speculations at the end when I was clearly half-awake, but at the point in the experience when I saw a definite visual image of the list of the French Ministry, I was certainly nearer the sleeping than the waking state.

Though it has taken some time to describe the general nature of this experience of sleep, the process of classifying it was very rapid in reality, and I proceeded almost at once to consider any events of the previous day which could have determined the manifest content.

I remembered clearly reading the list of the new French Ministry in the newspaper of the preceding day, and that I had been especially interested in the absence from it of Briand's name. During the day I had met an old Cambridge man who had asked me about the state of the University during the war, and this conversation would have tended to arouse the memory of the friend whose letter I had read in the dream. On the previous day I had also received the *Cambridge Magazine* of 17th March, containing an account of the attack which was being made on the Magazine at the time and of the measures by which the attack was being met, and at intervals during the day I had read extracts from the foreign journals which formed the especial feature of the paper at this time. I had been especially struck by the line taken by certain French journalists that the economic crippling of Germany was incompatible with the extraction of any indemnity from her in case of a successful conclusion of the war. This material seemed to have been utilised in the dream and to have influenced my speculations concerning the probable effects of the change of Ministry in France.

The day before the dream had thus provided plenty of material which would have determined the general lines of the sleeping experience. Much of this experience, however, was only very doubtfully of the nature of a dream. The part of the experience which was certainly a dream was reading the letter from my Cambridge friend, and therefore I turned my attention especially to this feature. As I have said, I could not remember its contents clearly, but the two points which stood out most prominently were its reproachful tone and the fact that the reproach was directed to my political views.

Several other dreams about this time seemed to have been determined by anxieties connected with my hospital work, and at this point in the analysis I turned to the medical experience of the previous day to find whether I had had any experience which could have made reproach the dominant affective element of the dream.

I had begun the previous morning feeling very tired and unfit for work, and had had an exceedingly busy day, through which I had only been carried by the interest of several cases and the belief that on the whole I had been able to deal with them successfully. The success of the day had, however, been marred by an incident at its close. Late in the evening I had been asked by a colleague to deal with a case of a very difficult kind, involving a disciplinary aspect. The situation was one of peculiar difficulty, and I had succeeded in carrying out the purpose desired by my colleague. But, though my conduct of the case had apparently been successful, I was acutely dissatisfied with it myself, for I had only succeeded through the application of a somewhat violent procedure, where milder measures might have been sufficient if I had shown more patience and forbearance. A successful day had thus ended with a feeling of dissatisfaction, and I had definitely reproached myself for what I counted as a failure.

The analysis thus led me to refer the reproachful character of the dream-letter to an affect of reproach which had been present in my mind shortly before going to bed. I was content with this interpretation and had not attempted to continue the analysis. At this time I had reached a point in the development of my views concerning the psychology of the dream when any confidence in Freud's views concerning the rôle of wish-fulfilment, which had been due to the "Presidency" dream, had been seriously undermined by later experience. I had been coming to the view that desire was not the only affective state by which a dream could be determined, but that dreams might be the expression of different affective states, such as fear, anxiety, shame, grief, etc. The especial interest of the dream to me at the moment was that the outstanding affective element of the manifest content had been reproach, and that reproach had been the outstanding feature of the experience of the period immediately preceding sleep. This dream had thus seemed to furnish striking confirmation of the view to which I was already being led, that dreams are attempts to express in sleep the affective state which is prominent in the dreamer's mind before going to sleep. At that time I had not formulated the view which I am adopting in this book, that dreams are the attempted solutions of conflicts.

Let us now turn to consider this dream and see how far it can be explained as a solution or attempted solution of a conflict. As I have already indicated, I regarded the political setting of the dream as having been determined by the contents of the *Cambridge Magazine* on the previous day. Taking the experience as a whole, I was inclined to regard it as an expression of a reproach arising out of my medical work, and was content to regard the difference in political opinion between my dream correspondent and myself as merely a feature of the manifest content by which the reproach had found expression.

If, however, we regard the incident of reading the letter as the dream proper, and the whole of the rest of the experience as half-waking, half-sleeping thoughts, to which we must look for the meaning of the dream, we are driven to conclude that the real factor determining the dream proper was a conflict arising in some way out of my attitude to the war. At the time I did not consider the dream from this point of view, for I was satisfied with the interpretation by which its content was referred to grounds for reproach arising out of an incident of my medical work. If, however, I am to adhere to the general principle of interpretation upon which this book is based, that the thoughts present in the half-waking state following a dream provide the clue to the thoughts by which the dream has been determined, we must regard a conflict connected with the war as the essential factor in the production of the dream. I was therefore driven to depart from my usual procedure and to undertake a new analysis when writing this chapter. In order to estimate the value of this analysis it must be remembered that it was made more than four years after the dream had taken place, and it is doubtful whether I should have thought it worthy of publication if the new analysis had not been made under conditions which are themselves of interest and illustrate the value of the thoughts immediately following a dream.

This chapter, up to the beginning of the last paragraph, was written on the morning of 29th July 1921, after which I proceeded to attempt a new analysis. In this I referred the dream to a conflict which I supposed might have been going on in my mind concerning the continuance of the war. At the time of the dream (1917) I was manifestly adopting the orthodox attitude, and any such pacifist tendency as might have been aroused by reading the *Cambridge Magazine* would have been repressed, thus providing exactly the conditions by which such a dream as that with which we are dealing would have been produced. I regarded the element of reproach as the affect which would naturally have come into action if in the dream-conflict the crude patriotic attitude had gained the advantage. During the following night (29th–30th July) I had a long and confused dream, of which, when I awoke, I remembered clearly only that I was going to my bedroom to have a siesta after lunch, taking with me books to read. On waking from this dream I found myself thinking about the problem of the day before, and then remembered clearly what I had then completely forgotten, that I had had a definite conflict in my mind at the time (*i.e.* March 1917) whether I was right in subscribing to the *Cambridge Magazine*. The conflict was between the view that it must be right to know the truth, to know what the people of other nations, enemy or allied, were thinking, and the view that in time of war nothing should be done to make people doubtful about the absolute justice of the cause for which they were fighting. In such a conflict there would be little question that the former attitude would appeal more to my adult intelligence, while the second point of view would have appealed more to me in youth. If I am right in supposing that in the dream infantile or youthful attitudes find expression, owing to the removal of higher restraining influences, the reproach which was the prominent affective feature of the dream would be natural to the youthful attitude which was finding expression in the dream.

The thoughts immediately following a dream which occurred four years after the analysis of another dream have thus led me to revise this analysis and to refer the earlier dream of reading the reproachful letter to a conflict arising out of the war, in place of regarding it as the expression of a reproach arising out of my medical work.

A question which remains is whether this professional reproach took any part in the causation of the dream, and whether the affect of reproach, which was manifestly present in my mind shortly before going to sleep, can have contributed to the reproach of the dream. The possibility that this may have been so, must certainly be kept in mind, though I do not think it is possible at present to form a decisive opinion. We need further evidence to show whether an affective state present in the mind of a person before going to sleep can reinforce or help to determine the occurrence of that affective state in a dream. (It must be noted that in the dream under consideration we have not to do with the occurrence in the dream of an affect of self-reproach, but of a reproachful tone on the part of a dream-personage. Though I was clearly aware of the reproachful character of the letter, I was not aware of experiencing in the dream any such state of self-reproach as clearly existed in the waking state before going to sleep.)

The analysis which I have just concluded was thus completed more than four years after the dream, as the result of half-waking thoughts reached after a second dream experienced while the later stage of the analysis was in progress.

I propose now to say something about this dream though, short as it is, I am unable to analyse it completely. In this dream I was going to my bedroom for a siesta, taking with me some books, and I had the impression that the books which I was taking to my bedroom were connected in some way with the *Cambridge Magazine*, though this impression was vague.* On seeking for an explanation of the manifest content, I remembered almost at once that I had read in the paper on the previous day that Mr Lloyd George had been advised to take a siesta after lunch, and was deriving great benefit from the practice. Mr Lloyd George was so intimately connected with the conduct of the war that it was natural that information concerning him should have been utilised to express a content in which the conduct of the war was intimately concerned. A recent experience of my own would also have tended to give the siesta after lunch a certain amount of prominence in my mind. A more important point is connected with the memory of the conflict about the *Cambridge Magazine*. In association with

* In connection with this, it may be mentioned that the *Cambridge Magazine* undertook the sale of books.

the act of taking these books to my bedroom I had the idea that it might have been right to read the Magazine in private, but that it was not suited for general circulation. This certainly fitted with an element in the old conflict, according to which it was thought that such knowledge as was being provided by the Magazine should be accessible, but that such accessibility had its dangers, especially in connection with the army, where it might lead to a lowering of *morale*. The bedroom of the dream thus seems to have served as a symbol for privacy as opposed to publicity in relation to this publication

This dream of "the reproachful letter" and its somewhat complicated analysis illustrates another point of great interest which I may consider here. In an earlier chapter I have mentioned the fact that according to Freud the wish of a patient to prove or disprove the views of his physician can provide the leading motive of a dream, and this suggests the danger that the theories of the dreamer may influence his dreams, leading them to provide evidence in favour of his views. I have had this possibility in mind from the time that I began to study dream-psychology, and have frequently made notes of facts which might help to determine how far this danger is real. In my original analysis of the dream of the reproachful letter there is a record of this kind. At the time that I had this dream I was reading *The Interpretation of Dreams* for the second time, and on 19th March I had read the final chapter of the book on the " Psychology of Dream Activities." When reading it, the thought had occurred to me that the danger of having his dreams influenced by his theories must be especially great in the case of one who had formulated so definite a theoretical position as that of Freud. I had wondered whether it might be possible to find evidence for such influence in any dream of mine. The sleep of the following night was, so far as I could tell, free from dreams, but the dream of the reproachful letter occurred on the following night. As I have already stated, I was at that time coming to question Freud's view that the dream is always a wish-fulfilment, and was coming to believe that it might be the expression of any affective state. At the end of my original analysis I comment on the fact that according to this analysis this dream was determined by an affect of self-reproach, and thus furnished confirmation of the theoretical view to which I was already inclining. The dream and its analysis thus seemed to support the view that the course of a dream might be determined by the theoretical interests of the dreamer. The result of the later analysis undertaken in this chapter, however, has been to show that the early analysis was wrong, or at least very incomplete. The reproach arising out of my medical work has been shown to have taken only a secondary place, the real motive being just a conflict of a political kind, such as was implied in the dream-letter. If the later analysis is accepted, any influence of my theoretical bias at the time had been on the analysis rather than on the dream itself. I have no doubt whatever that it was only my theoretical interest in the view that the dream might be the expression of any kind of affective state which led me to be satisfied with an analysis which referred the dream to a state of self-reproach, and led me to pay no attention to the conflict which was revealed four years later by the thoughts following another dream. I suggest, therefore, that, so far as this dream is concerned, it shows clearly how the theories of a dreamer may influence his self-analysis, but provides no evidence that they influence his dreams. The dream and its analysis have more bearing on the methodology of the self-analysis of the dream than on the theory of the dream itself, and reveal clearly one of the dangers of such self-analysis.

CONSTRUCTIVE FUNCTION OF THE DREAM

There is little question that problems may be solved in sleep which either have not previously been the object of serious attempts at solution or may even have been beyond the powers of the sleeper when awake. In such cases it is often difficult to obtain any light upon the nature of the process by which the problem was solved. As often happens, cases in which the constructive function is less obvious and less complete may be of more value in enabling us to recognise the kind of process by which such results are obtained.

A good example of a constructive function of this kind is provided by the "cup and saucer" dream reported in Chapter III, in which a problem concerning the distribution of patients in the different rooms of a hospital was suggested by a dream, the dream-consciousness having apparently utilised a piece of information, the importance of which had not been realised in the waking state. The dream-consciousness had formulated, though only in symbolic form, a solution of which the waking consciousness had not been capable.

THE "HIDDEN SOURCES" DREAM

I propose now to relate a dream of my own which illustrates the kind of way in which the constructive function is exerted. In this dream, which occurred during the night of 24th–25th March 1917, I was reading a paper in what I took to be the *Southern Cross Log*, the monthly publication of the Melanesian Mission, in which a missionary was writing about the people of some island, either in the Banks group or the New Hebrides. He was referring to the fact that the natives of this island were quite ignorant of any such history of the origin of their stonework as I had put forward in my book *The History of Melanesian Society*. The writer spoke of this with regret, owing to its seeming failure to support the value of " hidden sources," to which, in common with myself, those working in Melanesia were coming to attach so much importance. I had the idea in the dream that " hidden sources " referred to survivals. The writer then passed on to regret that my views concerning such matters were practically dead.

In this dream I saw the print distinctly, but not the whole page. At the same time there was a distinct visual image, which appeared to be detached from the printed page, of a pattern of lines which I took to represent stonework. The stones had sharp outlines as if carefully carved and placed in close apposition to one another, so that in some respects the image resembled a design for weaving or plaiting rather than a representation of stonework. It was certainly very different from any stonework found in Melanesia. I woke from this dream more or less suddenly, without any obvious half-waking stage, and wrote down the dream before the analysis began.

The first thought which came to me was that during the preceding evening I had read a paper on " Tüba-tulabal and Kawaiisu Kinship Terms," by E. W. Gifford,* which had reached me on that day from America. In the paper there had been several refer-ences to the dependence of kinship nomenclature upon forms of marriage in which I am especially interested. These references had been brief and one was of a kind which, though probably not intended by the author, might have been regarded as contemptuous. I may have been annoyed by this, but what had interested

* University of California Publications in American Archæology and Ethnology, Berkeley, U.S.A., Vol. XII, page 219, 1917.

me far more was that, failing to recognise the dependence of kinship terms upon forms of marriage as only part of the much wider thesis of regarding these terms as an expression of the social organisation, the author had paid no attention to facts which seemed to me to afford striking evidence in favour of my views. I had therefore finished the paper highly pleased at having been provided with evidence in favour of my views—evidence all the more satisfactory in that it could not be due to any bias on the part of the collector of the information, for he had completely missed its bearing. Between reading the paper and going to bed I had been subjected to one or two annoying experiences and, being very tired, my general mood was depressed on going to sleep. Consequently, when the analysis was made, I was inclined to regard the reference to my views being practically dead as an expression of an attitude of depression connected with my anthropological work, and of my annoyance at the real nature of my views concerning the relation of kinship and social organisation having been misunderstood.

I could recall no special event during the preceding day which would have called my attention to Melanesia, but the peculiarity of nomenclature which had especially interested me in Gifford's paper was characteristic of certain Melanesian systems of relationship, and would certainly have taken my thoughts in that direction. Moreover, a copy of the *Southern Cross Log* was lying on a table in my room and had probably been observed during the day.

The feature which stood out with especial prominence when I recalled the dream was the reference to " hidden sources." I had the idea clearly in the dream that this expression referred to survivals, and it was only at a late stage of the analysis that it occurred to me that it was an unusual way of regarding survivals to speak of them as " hidden sources." The doctrine of survival is very prominent in my anthropological work, the whole of my theoretical construction based on the nomenclature of kinship resting upon the idea that kinship terms are survivals of earlier forms of social organisation. There would thus be a definite connection between " hidden sources " and the thoughts aroused by reading Gifford's paper.

It then occurred to me that "hidden sources " would also be an appropriate expression for facts prominent in my mind at the time through my growing interest in the work of Freud that the unconscious is a store of "hidden sources " of knowledge. So far as I am aware, it had not previously occurred to me that there was any similarity between the " survivals " of anthropology and the unconscious experience which bulks so largely in the Freudian psychology. It had never occurred to me that a kinship term used by a people who had no idea that it reveals their past history might be regarded as a hidden source of knowledge comparable with a piece of unconscious experience. Though the resemblance implies nothing more than an analogy, it is one of those analogies which enables us the better to understand the two kinds of experience brought into relation with one another. The analogy of a social survival with a fossil is one with which I was already familiar, and a fossil is pre-eminently a " hidden source " of know-ledge, but that a social survival might be regarded as a " hidden source " of knowledge had not previously occurred to me.

So far I have been content to explain the occurrence of the " hidden sources " of the dream and have sug-gested that this expression points to a resemblance or analogy between two very different things which had not occurred to me when awake. I may now consider this dream from another point of view, with the aim of discovering whether we can discern the kind of process by which the dream-consciousness reached this construction. The dream occurred at a time when I was coming to the conclusion that dreams might be the expression of any affective state prominent in the mind of the dreamer at the time. It occurred four nights after the dream of the reproachful letter, which seemed to me at the time to provide such good evidence for the truth of the view which was then being formulated in my mind. It was therefore natural that I should have been content to regard the conclusion expressed at the end of the dream that my views were practically dead as due to the state of depression present before I went to sleep. At that time I had not reached the view that dreams are attempted solutions of conflicts. Let us now inquire how far it is possible to look upon this dream of " hidden sources " from this point of view.

Though I made no reference to the fact in my original analysis, there is no question that at the time I was the subject of a definite conflict between interests in ethnology and psychology. During the earlier part of my medical service during the war, my main intellectual interest continued to be in ethnology, and until the beginning of 1917 my spare time was devoted to work on that subject. It was only after I began work in Scotland that my growing interest in the psychological problems suggested by war-neurosis began to compete and conflict with my interest in ethnology. I believe that this conflict formed a definite factor in the " pacifist " dream, and my desire to return to my ethnological work took an important part in the egoistic motive which led to my wish that the war should end at all costs. If, as I can be confident was the case, this conflict was present at the time, there is no question that it would have been stimulated by reading Gifford's paper. This paper contained facts which were not only of great interest in themselves, but they also provided important arguments in favour of my views concerning the scientific problem which forms perhaps my most important contribution to ethnology. Moreover, there was a special motive of an egoistic kind which would have led me to wish to carry on the line of work suggested by Gifford's paper. At this time several American ethnologists were disagreeing with my views and especially with their applicability to American society. Common to all of them was a misunderstanding of an important part of my position, which, although clearly stated in my book, had been neglected. Gifford's paper, on the day preceding the dream, had provided evidence in my favour, and the fact that it had been provided by an American worker who obviously disbelieved in my position, provided a controversial opportunity which one would be sorry to miss. Nevertheless, I knew that I could only avail myself of this opportunity by withdrawing from my psychological work the small amount of spare time for writing which was then available. I do not think that it requires much imagination to see how strong such a conflict would be and how naturally, if my general views are correct, it would become the groundwork of a dream.

Let us now consider the dream in more detail to discover how far it provides a solution, successful or unsuccessful, of the conflict. If my interpretation is right, the dream forms a good example of condensation. The expression " hidden sources " was found to point to the recognition by the dream-consciousness of a similarity between a kinship term and a fragment of unconscious experience. The expression brought into relation with one another the two interests which were conflicting with one another. It affords a good example of a compromise-formation in which the dream-consciousness pointed the way to a means of reconciliation which had not occurred to me in the waking state.

It was only later that I came to see that there was no real conflict between ethnology and psychology, but that the two studies are mutually helpful, and that such knowledge of the two as had come to me formed an opportunity to be utilised, and later in the year I prepared the lecture *Dreams and Primitive Culture,** which forms the first of a series of papers in which I have dealt with the extensive border-region between psychology and ethnology.

If I am right, this dream was an example of the constructive function of the dream in that the expression " hidden sources " refers to a resemblance or analogy which had not presented itself to the waking consciousness. I must now inquire whether we can discover any reason why this analogy should have occurred in sleep rather than in the waking state ; why in this respect the state of sleep should have shown itself superior to the waking life. I do not think it is difficult to find the answer. In sleep the conflict between ethnology and psychology was free and open. There was no process of repression in activity to keep the conflict out of sight and restrain one or other of the two contestants. The egoistic motive which urged me not only to go on with my ethnological work, but also to avail myself of an opportunity to demolish opponents, was not checked and thwarted by the more altruistic motive that it was now my business to understand and apply the principles of psycho-therapy. The two interests had equal play, so that the imagination could apply itself without restraint to find a solution for the conflict.

One other element may be discerned in the solution. The expression " hidden sources " refers only to an analogy. In my adult state I distrust analogies, and the mere fact that the resemblance suggested by the dream is nothing more than an analogy would, in the

* *Bull. John Rylands Library,* 1917.

adult waking state, have aroused distrust and consequent repression. It is probable that this forms another motive for the occurrence in sleep of a means of solving my conflict which had not occurred to me when awake.

I have dealt with this case at length because, though the problem attacked and solved by the dream-consciousness is comparatively trivial and unimportant, I believe that it points the way to the explanation of the more serious constructive accomplishments, of which sleep may be the scene. In this case the consciousness of sleep succeeded in pointing the way to a mode of reconciling two conflicting interests, partly because there was no inhibition or repression, partly because the solution was of the nature of an analogy which was not acceptable to the scientific attitude of the waking state. I suggest that these two factors, and especially the former, may be responsible for those cases in which, in sleep, people have written poems or accomplished other works of art. This suggests that poems composed in sleep, and such accomplishments, as the solving of mathematical or other problems in sleep, should be more carefully scrutinised than has hitherto been customary, with the object of discovering whether the sleeping consciousness has not utilised processes, such as analogy and simile, which would have been distrusted in the waking state.

One other feature of the dream must be considered. The dream ended with an expression of regret on the part of the dream-writer that my views concerning the stonework of Melanesia were practically dead. In my original analysis I took this to be an expression of the depressed mood present before I went to bed. The dream not only ended with the statement that my views were dead, but it also expressed regret that my views concerning " hidden sources " were not confirmed. These parts of the dream seem to suggest that in spite of its constructive effort the dream was, nevertheless, a failure of solution. When considering the dream of the reproachful letter I mentioned the possibility that, though this dream could be explained as the result of a conflict, the affect which was dominant in it may have been due to the attitude of reproach present before going to sleep that had taken so prominent a place in my first attempt at analysis. The despondent tone of the present dream seems to point definitely in the same direction. It suggests that though dreams are the attempted solutions of conflicts, the nature of the solution is largely determined by the affective attitude dominant before going to sleep

CHAPTER IX

DREAM AND PSYCHO-NEUROSIS

UNTIL now I have been considering the psychology of the dream, quite apart from its relation to other products of mental activity. I propose in this chapter to deal—it can only be very briefly—with some of these relations. The dream, or perhaps more correctly, different varieties of the dream, occupy an intermediate position between certain forms of mental activity universally regarded as pathological, and others which are not only regarded as normal and healthy, but as products of the human mind, so valuable that they might be regarded as supernormal, rather than subnormal or abnormal. I propose now to consider the relation of the dream to certain pathological mental processes on the one hand, and to the products of artistic and religious activity on the other hand.

It has been one of the chief arguments of this book that dreams are attempts to solve in sleep conflicts which are disturbing the waking life. I have referred the character of the dream, at any rate in so far as its emotional aspect is concerned, to the degree in which this attempted solution is successful. Those who have read my book *Instinct and the Unconscious* will have recognised that I have been trying to bring dreams within a formula closely comparable with that by which I have in that book explained the psychoses and psycho-neuroses. These are regarded as attempts, successful or unsuccessful, so far as the patient's comfort is concerned, to solve conflicts which are disturbing the normal course of life. When the solution is successful, as in the state which I have taken as the characteristic example of hysteria, there is no affect. When the solution is wholly unsuccessful, as in anxiety-neurosis, there is affect and of a painful kind. Moreover, just as it is possible to consider many forms of dream as the simple fulfilments of a wish, in a symbolic form which satisfies the level of the mind that is active in the degree of sleep in which the dream occurs, so is it possible to regard the hysterical paralysis or mutism as the unwitting fulfilment of a wish for some occurrence which will remove the subject of a mental conflict from the scene of that conflict. We may even, in many cases, regard the paralysis or mutism as having a symbolic nature, as being a symbol of the more complete suppression of all movement of which I have supposed the hysterical disability to be a manifestation. Attempts have been made to show an even closer similarity between the dream and hysteria, and to find processes in the production of the hysterical symptom that correspond to those by which the latent dream-thoughts find expression in the manifest dream. Thus, as I have already indicated, even the simple hysterical paralysis may be regarded as an example of symbolisation, and this character is still more obvious in many cases of civilian hysteria where, in place of the crude paralysis or anæsthesia, the symptoms are of a more elaborate kind in which they symbolise, or seem to symbolise, the situation from which the patient wishes to escape. The next character, that of dramatisation, is more obvious. Hysteria may be regarded as a prolonged drama, in which the sufferer leads, perhaps for years, a life of an artificial kind, by which he or she escapes from a conflict with a situation of real life. In this mode of solving the conflict, the element of make-believe enters in a manner closely comparable with that which forms an essential part of a dramatic situation. Hysteria may be regarded as an unwitting simulation, and thus resembles the simulation of situations of real life, which is an essential part of the drama. Condensation again is often evident in the production of the hysterical symptom. Factors of the most various kinds, which enter into the conflict, may find their expression in a mutism or other simple form of hysterical disability.

Displacement again occurs in a form closely comparable with that to which Freud assigns so important a place in the production of the dream, so closely, indeed, as to lead one to suspect that the weight laid upon displacement by Freud, in his theoretical consideration of the dream, was suggested by his experience with hysteria, for it must always be remembered that the whole of Freud's construction starts from hysteria, and that a tendency can always be discerned in his work whereby this is the pattern to which other mental mechanisms, normal or abnormal, are made to conform.

These various characters are even more strikingly present if we compare the dream with the disorder known as compulsion-neurosis. In this disease the sufferer has an overwhelming drive to perform certain acts, sometimes of a simple kind, but often very complex, which, while they satisfy a craving if carried out, give rise to the most intense discomfort if their performance is not allowed.

In this case psycho-analytic investigations have shown clearly that the compulsive acts are of a definitely symbolic kind. They are symbolic acts whereby a person satisfies wishes or cravings in an unwitting manner. This is especially clear in the ritual, often of a highly complex kind, which, in many persons, may accompany the act of going to bed. The various acts of arranging the bed and bed-clothes in a certain manner or other features are almost certainly symbols by means of which a conflict is unwittingly satisfied. Their dramatic quality is still more obvious, and they may be equally regarded as examples of condensation and displacement. In these two cases of hysteria and compulsion-neurosis, the conflict of the real life is satisfied by these symbolic expressions, and so long as the hysterical manifestation or the performance of the compulsive act is not interfered with, the painful affect natural to the conflict is absent, though the solution itself is liable to produce new conflicts by its incompatibility with the social surroundings of the sufferer.

While in these two examples the solution is, or may be, so successful as to lead to absence of affect, psycho-neurosis may be accompanied by painful and even highly exaggerated affect, just as the dream may be so accompanied.

In the discussion of " Affect in the Dream " (Chapter V), I have regarded the nightmare and other such painful dreams as those of my suicidal patient (Chapter II) as failures to solve the conflict upon which the nightmare or dream depends, and that I ascribe the painful character of the affect to this failure. I believe that the case is exactly the same in the disorder we call anxiety-neurosis. This is a psycho-neurosis, accompanied by painful affect, and there is every reason to believe that the special features of the disease depend upon a conflict, present in the patient's mind, which wholly fails of solution. There is the further striking feature that prominent among the symptoms of anxiety-neurosis are nightmares and unpleasant dreams. The close similarity between the unpleasant dreams and states of anxiety-neurosis is well illustrated by a dream of my own, which occurred during the last year of the war, when I was living within a hundred yards of the great gun at Hampstead. One night I awoke with the report of the gun, and while listening to the varied sounds of the raid, thought that I distinguished one which might have been caused by the bursting of a bomb. Then I found myself in a room, sitting by a bed, with my head, face downwards, pressed against the bed. I was aware that there was the danger of a bomb and that the room was near the roof, and I looked up with definite apprehension. I was reproaching myself for showing fear in an air-raid, when I realised that the room in which I had just been present was not my own and that the experience had been a dream. The apprehension had either gone as soon as I awoke, or went as soon as I realised that I had been dreaming, and I became at once extremely interested in the experience through which I had just passed. I recognised it as fitting in a beautiful manner with my theory of the rôle of repression in connection with the nightmare. There can be little doubt that when I distinguished the sound which I took to be that of a bursting bomb, I had had a tendency towards fear, which I had repressed, and that on going to sleep this fear, repressed in the waking state, had found expression in the apprehension of the dream. On going into the details of the dream I remembered an occasion on which I had looked upwards during an earlier air-raid. I had sat through a performance at the Coliseum during an air-raid, and on looking upwards had noticed that I was sitting immediately under the dome, with its obvious suggestion of possibilities. During this speculation about the nature and causes of my apprehension I went to sleep again and had a second dream, the details of which I remembered clearly when I awoke, but rapidly forgot, as I did not record them at once. The important point, however, is that it was wholly free from any unpleasant affect. I then went to sleep again, and slept through the rest of the raid without waking.

The interest of the first dream is that it may be

regarded as a miniature psycho-neurosis lasting only a minute or two and cured completely, also in a minute or so, by the procedure I was accustomed to employ in treating cases of anxiety-neurosis. I have no doubt that if on waking I had been ashamed, as indeed I was for a moment, and had repressed the fear and shame, and had tried to persuade myself that I had not been afraid, I should have had a second dream of which the nightmare character would have been more definite, or I might even have started an anxiety-neurosis, for at that time all the conditions, such as fatigue and impaired physical health, which would have predisposed to the occurrence of a psycho-neurosis, were definitely present. Instead of this, the occurrence of fear in sleep became at once, on awaking, an object of scientific interest, and this interest removed at once all danger of repression and all occasion for the occurrence of shame. My attitude provided an admirable, though as a matter of fact unwitting, example of the psycho-therapeutic principles which at that time I was seeking to formulate. I was at the time so interested in the rôle of repression in the production of the symptoms of psycho-neurosis that on thinking about the dream only this aspect occurred to me. The dream also fits in with the formula that dreams are attempts to solve conflicts; in this case an unsuccessful solution, as indicated by the accompaniment of unpleasant affect. In this connection I must refer to a condition of a conflict which I have not so far mentioned. There were many people living in the house, all of whom, with the exception of myself, were in the habit of getting up whenever there was an air-raid, and assembling in one of the lower rooms of the house. I believe that when I thought on this occasion I had detected the sound of a bomb, I may have been tempted to follow the general example.

The chief interest of this dream is that it illustrates

so well the resemblance between a dream and a psycho-neurosis that it may be regarded as a miniature psycho-neurosis, the whole course of which, including its successful treatment, lasted only a few minutes. It not only illustrates the part taken in the production both of dreams and psycho-neuroses by repression, as well as the mechanisms common to both, but it also serves as an example of the general principle that both are the attempted solutions of conflicts, as well as of the further principle that the nature and intensity of the affect depends upon the degree in which the attempted solution is successful.

Another general formula put forward in this book is that the dream is an example of regression. Here again the formula corresponds exactly with one which holds good for psycho-neurosis. In Chapter XVIII of *Instinct and the Unconscious* I have considered many forms of psycho-neurosis and psychosis from this point of view, and have tried to show that all their manifestations can be regarded as regressions to earlier forms of mental functioning and to instinctive reactions, many of which never become manifest in healthy adult life.

Another feature of the dream upon which I have tried to insist in this book falls closely into line with one which, according to my belief, holds good of the psycho-neuroses. All the dreams which I have analysed have been referred to recent conflicts in the life of the sleeper. Though many dreams and many features of dreams require for their complete explanation conditions going back to the early life of the dreamer, states determined by heredity, and even happenings with which the dreamer as an individual has had nothing to do, it has been possible to explain every feature, even of long and complex dreams, by the nature of conflicts in the recent experience of the dreamer. The conclusion has been drawn that Freud and the psycho-analytic school generally have greatly exaggerated the part taken by infantile experience in the causation of the dream. The view put forward in this book is that while the dream is essentially a mode of regressive mental functioning, a regression to the ways of early life, the experience which is embodied in the dream, upon which the dream-processes act, is derived from the recent experience of the dreamer.

I believe that an exactly similar situation holds good of mental disorder, and that in this department, as in the psychology of the dream, the importance of early experience has been greatly exaggerated by Freud and his followers. Evidence seems to be accumulating that the special " complexes," or other special forms of infantile experience, to which so great a rôle has been ascribed in the causation of the psycho-neuroses, belong to the mental make-up of everyone. If they are the essential causes of mental disorder, we have to explain why some people suffer from psycho-neuroses and others escape. Factors universal in mankind cannot be regarded as the essential causes, though they may take their part in determining the special forms which mental disorders in general take. The tendency of the psycho-analytic school to accentuate the importance of the early factors, and the accompanying neglect of the part taken by recent conflicts, seem to me to be of exactly the same order as the attitude of the same school towards the dream. In both cases we have to distinguish a highly complex chain of causation. The recent history of the study of both dream and psycho-neurosis seems to reveal a similar tendency to lay undue stress on early factors and a relative neglect of recent conflicts, which I believe to be far more influential in the production of both dream and psycho-neurosis than is now usually supposed.

DREAM AND PSYCHO-NEUROSIS

DREAM AND MYTH

I can now turn to the relation of the dream to artistic and religious activity. If I am right in regarding the dream as a regression, it is evident that we must seek for its points of resemblance with artistic production to the earlier and cruder forms of this activity. Though it is possible, if not probable, that even in the highest developments of artistic production there are points of resemblance with the dream, it is with the earlier forms of these activities, such as the myth, that we should expect to find the resemblance especially definite and far-reaching. It is therefore not surprising that the relation of the dream to the myth is a subject which has already been frequently considered by the psycho-analytic school.

In the numerous writings on this subject, which we owe to Freud and his followers, far more attention has been paid to the content of the myth than to the processes by which the myth comes into being. Following the general trend of psycho-analytic writings, the chief aim of workers has been to prove that just as most dreams and all psycho-neuroses are believed to have a sexual basis, so are sexual motives believed to play the chief, if not the only, part in the origin and development of myths.

The mechanisms of myth-production have, however, been by no means neglected, and here again, following Freud, it has been customary to regard myths as the fulfilment of wishes. Thus, according to Karl Abraham, one of the first to follow Freud in this region, the myth contains in disguised form the wishes of the childhood of the race. This disguise is believed to be effected by processes of condensation and displacement exactly comparable with those of the dream-mechanism, while the concept of the censorship is freely drawn upon in the attempts to show how these processes have been in action.

It is impossible within the limits of this book to attempt to treat this subject adequately, and I propose to content myself with a few points of resemblance between the dream and the myth, as illustrated by dreams already related or referred to in this book.

One of the most general features of early mythology is the tendency to personify natural objects, and to regard these objects, such as hills, rivers, trees, etc., as having such human characteristics as the power of speech. It is therefore of interest that in what I have called the transference dream of my patient, narrated in the second chapter, the river sang to the dreamer to swim on his journey and take courage, an incident of a kind which repeatedly occurs in the myths of primitive peoples. We have reason to believe that in the dream this human behaviour of the river was directly connected with the identification of the natural objects with a human being, that the river of the dream was the symbol or representative of a person, and it is probable * that, at the stage of social development, of which myth-formation is especially characteristic, there is a similar identification, and that every natural object to which man's attention is especially directed is thought of as having human characteristics, and is

---

* If Dr Rivers had been able to prepare the manuscript of this book for publication it is unlikely that he would have left these statements concerning the comparison of dreams and myths in their present form. His attitude toward the general problem is clearly expounded in his Presidential Address to the Folk-lore Society (" The Symbolism of Rebirth," *Folk-lore*, March 1922) ; and after having formulated his views so definitely it is inconceivable that he would have permitted the crude animism to which he seems to subscribe on this page to have gone forth as his real opinion. Nor do I think he would have left his statements concerning the sexual factor in the development of myths (page 152) in their present form without further explanation and qualification. Therefore I have added a brief note (Appendix II) calling attention to certain considerations which he might have set forth if he had revised his manuscript himself.—G. E. S.

endowed with such human characters as the power of speech and the capacity for locomotion. That animals should talk is just as natural to the man of lowly culture as it is natural to the dream-consciousness of the most highly civilised of mankind.

Another feature of the same dream may be noted. I will quote the part of the dream to which I have already referred: " The river was friendly and sang to me to continue on my journey and take courage. I did so, and felt happy, and could take powerful strokes with ease."

The point to which I wish to call attention here is that nothing is said in the account of diving or other means of getting into the river, but it is natural to the dreamer that he should at one moment be walking by the river bank and at the next taking powerful strokes. Transitions of this kind are in my experience habitual in the narrations of the people we call savage, especially in their myths. At one moment a narrator will be talking about a man and at the next moment he will speak of his settling on the bough of a tree, as if it were a perfectly natural thing to do, it being quite unnecessary to make any reference to the transformation into a bird which, from our point of view, is needed to make the action of the story intelligible. Everyone who thinks of the natural and easy transitions of his dreams from one situation to another cannot fail to recognise the probability that such transitions are equally natural to man in the mythopœic stage of his development.

Another interesting point of similarity between the dream and the myth or other product of the savage mind is the composite nature of their objects. One of the most common experiences of the dream is the appearance of a composite image of a person in which it is possible to distinguish two or more different personalities. Thus, in a dream of my own (reported in Chapter X), which depended on a conflict concerning a pacifist attitude, there is a good example of such a composite personality of two professors, each of whom personified an aspect of the conflict, that character predominating which was in agreement with the nature of the solution which was being expressed by the dream. Similar composite creatures are very prominent in early myth and belief, though composite animals or creatures made up of man and animal are more frequent than in the dream of the civilised person. An excellent example of such a composite creature is the dragon, which resembles in many respects the composite formation of a dream.*

DREAM AND POEM

While many may be ready to acknowledge the similarity of dream and myth, the proposition that the mechanism of the production of poetry is closely similar to that of the dream will awaken more opposition. There is little doubt, however, that this similarity exists. It is possible to take the images of the manifest content of a poem and discover more or less exactly how each has been suggested by the experience, new or old, of the poet. It is also possible, at any rate in many cases, to show how these images are symbolic expressions of some conflict which is raging in the mind of the poet, and that the real underlying meaning or latent content of the poem is very different from that which the outward imagery would suggest. Moreover, it is possible to show the occurrence of a process of condensation by means of which many different experiences are expressed by means of a simple image. There is also a striking resemblance with other products considered in this book in that the

* G. Elliot Smith, *The Evolution of the Dragon*, Manchester, 1919.

poem may come in a state closely resembling a dissociation from the experience of ordinary life.

I cannot give you direct evidence for this, for the obvious reason that, unfortunately, I am not a poet. Just as I believe that a really satisfactory analysis of a dream is only possible to the dreamer himself or to one who knows the conflicts and experiences of the dreamer in a most unusual way, so do I believe that only when poets and other artists have set to work to analyse the products of their artistry can we expect to understand the real mechanism of artistic production.

In this comparison of the poem with the dream, one fact must be emphasised. The poem as we read it is very rarely the immediate product of the poetic activity, but has been the subject of a lengthy process of a critical kind, comparable with that which Freud has called the secondary elaboration of the dream. It is only through the study of the immediate unelaborated product of the poet's mind that we can expect to understand the part of the process of artistic production which is comparable with the formation of the dream.

CONTENT AND MECHANISM

In the consideration of the psychology of the dream, of which I have attempted a brief sketch in this book, and in the still more brief consideration of other products of mental activity, which I have attempted in this chapter, I have been dealing especially with the mechanisms or processes by which these different products of mental activity come into being. I have said little about the nature of the material upon which these mechanisms or processes work, and build it up, it may be, into the airy and fantastic dream ; or into the equally fantastic if less airy behaviour of the subject of a compulsion-neurosis ; or into the measured imagery of a poem.

Before I close I should like to say a word about the content of these different forms of activity.

The dreams which I have related in this book have been carried back to contents of various kinds. In one dream this content was concerned with the conflicting emotions generated by doubts concerning the acceptance of an honour ; in another was deeply involved the instinct of self-preservation as brought into action by the presence of a situation so terrible that to the subject of the conflict there seemed no remedy but suicide ; in another dream the conflict was between a simple wish for change and for the satisfaction of interests which, though taking the guise of science, were really nothing more than manifestations of the instinct of curiosity on the one hand, and social sentiments of duty towards others.

These dreams conflict with the opinion generally ascribed to Freud and his followers that dreams have usually or always a sexual content. That dreams may have such a content, and have such content very frequently, stands beyond all doubt, but for obvious reasons one does not choose them when the object is to illustrate the mechanisms and processes of dream-production. I trust that the dreams I have related will be sufficient to show that all dreams have not this content, and that any conflict which is capable of disturbing the even tenor of Man's life may serve as the motive of a dream. I should like further to say that in this opinion I am in agreement with Freud himself. Not only do most of the dreams he relates and analyses depend on other than sexual motives, but in the last edition of the *Traumdeutung*, he states explicitly that neither in that edition nor in any earlier edition will the reader find any support for the view that dreams are wholly determined by motives of a sexual kind. That extravagance is only one among the many extravagances which we owe to indiscriminating zeal with which the followers of Freud have outrun their master, and thereby brought a great contribution to knowledge into disrepute.

In the similar views concerning the nature of the factors which underlie the production of psychoneurosis Freud himself cannot be acquitted from blame, though such a mistake is not unnatural if attention be limited exclusively to the disorders customary in the ordinary life of civilised society in which the sexual instinct is more than any other the subject of unregulated repressions and suppressions. The experience of the war has now, however, convinced most students of the subject that the equally fundamental, or even more fundamental, instinct of self-preservation must be put side by side with the sexual instinct as the starting-point for the development of psycho-neurosis, and it is probable that, when attention is directed to it, the instinct of self-preservation will be found to play a far more important rôle in the production of the neuroses of civil life than most psycho-analysts are yet ready to recognise.

Mythology and magical or religious rite already have a history long enough to allow a forecast of what we may expect to happen in other branches of mental activity. Anthropology has already passed through the phase in which to every strange rite and belief of the different peoples of the earth was ascribed a sexual, or, as it was called, a phallic, motive. This was followed by a later phase in which, perhaps as a reaction against the sexual interest, students ascribed all myths to an interest largely of an intellectual kind— the interest in the movements and changes in appearance of sun, moon and stars, and especially in Germany many mythologists came to believe exclusively in these motives as others had believed as exclusively in motives of a sexual kind. Strangely enough, it is only since the war, and as the result of the discovery of the great part which the instinct of self-preservation plays in the production of mental disorder that we are beginning to recognise the vast part which this instinct has taken in the determination of savage belief and custom. We are now coming to see to how great an extent uncertainties concerning the supply of food, and especially the need for rain as the necessary condition of an abundant food supply, have taken in the determination of the magical and religious beliefs and practices of mankind. In all the early civilisations, in Asia, in Africa, in Oceania, and in America, a foremost place was given to magical and religious rites for the production of the rain which is so essential to the satisfaction of the instincts of nutrition.

Again, under the leading of Elliot Smith * we are coming to believe in the enormous importance of the desire for the lengthening of life as a motive for some of the most striking beliefs and customs of mankind. It is possible, perhaps probable, that our interest in these and other motives has led us to neglect the part which motives of a sexual kind have taken in the growth of mythology and religion. These motives are quite clearly to be discerned in some of the more advanced religions, and are especially obvious in certain of the developments of the religions of India. It may be that in the study of the ruder beliefs and customs of mankind, the pendulum has swung too far, and that sexual factors have been more important than we now suppose.†

---

* *The Evolution of the Dragon*, Manchester, 1919.

† It is important to discriminate between the sexual act and the process of reproduction or life-giving. The earliest religious ideas are associated with the concept of life-giving, not merely in the literal sense of birth or rebirth, but also of prolonging life, renewing youth, averting death, or attaining success in love and sport. In other words, the motive underlying the most primitive form of religion, which is preserved in myth, is the worship of the Great

DREAM AND PSYCHO-NEUROSIS

I need not refer here to the varied nature of the content of poetry and of other products of artistic activity. All the forms of activity which have been brought into relation with the dream agree with it in being capable of arising through the action of any agencies which may set up a conflict in the mind. The dream is just as little determined solely by motives arising out of sex as motives of this kind are solely responsible for the morbid processes of psycho-neurosis and for the products of artistic and religious activity.

PRACTICAL VALUE OF THE STUDY OF DREAMS

If I am right that the dream affords a guide to the nature of psycho-neurosis, and that the study of the dream confirms the importance of recent conflicts in the production of psycho-neurosis, it will follow that in psycho-therapeutic treatment especial attention should be paid to recent conflicts by facing these conflicts and learning the means by which they may be solved. We may acknowledge that for a complete understanding of the conflict, and of the personality of the patient as an essential element in the conflict, a deeper analysis may be necessary, but there are many cases in which, for reason of time or money or other cause, the acquisition of such deeper knowledge is not practicable, and much can be done by a more

Mother or Giver of Life; and it is an expression of the instinct of self-preservation rather than that of sex. But once the organs of reproduction came to symbolise the life-giving powers, and especially when the phallus replaced the female organ as the more important religious symbol, it was inevitable that its potency as a life-giver should be overshadowed by its attributes as the instrument of sexual gratification. What I want to emphasise here is that the rôle of the sexual instinct in the development of religion, myth and folk-tale, is not primary but secondary to the craving for a life-giving elixir. The recognition of this unquestionable fact destroys the foundations of the speculations of Freud, Jung and their followers. In his zeal to build a bridge which will bring the Freudians and the ethnologists together, Dr Rivers has used ambiguous phrases, which suggest views that are contrary to his real beliefs.—G. E. S.

complete dealing with the recent conflict which serves as the immediate cause of the morbid state. Even in a very small experience I have met with cases in which it has seemed to me that in their enthusiasm for the discovery of factors dating back to childhood, psycho-analysts have neglected obvious recent conflicts, or have not given them sufficient weight.*

I do not propose here to say anything about the value of the dream in psycho-analysis proper. There is no doubt that the dream and associations arising out of the dream can provide the means of getting back to early experience and to morbid elements of this experience. I propose here to consider only the clinical value of dream-analyses of the kind I have described in this book. I shall only deal with the question whether dream-analysis has value when one is content with getting back to the recent conflicts which are serving as the immediate conditions of dream or psycho-neurosis, or both.

It might seem at first sight that such analysis of the dreams of others as I have utilised in this book may be of little clinical value. If I am right that one is only justified in using the dreams of others as material for the scientific study of dreams, when one has extensive knowledge of the personality of the dreamer and of the conflicts by which his life is being disturbed, it might seem that the dream can be of little use practically. It is necessary, however, here to distinguish between value as scientific evidence and clinical value, two very different things. I have given you one striking example of the clinical value of the dream

---

* Dr Rivers had intended to compare this tendency in psychological practice with the recent history of ethnological speculation, and to refer especially to the way in which the true and obvious meaning of certain groups of facts has so often been overlooked by those who were intent on discovering some more elusive explanation in the mistaken belief that they were interpreting the evidence in accordance with the principles of evolution.

in what I call the suicide dream. Here I was able to analyse the dream at once, owing to my knowledge of the dreamer, and it may be useful to inquire exactly in what the utility of that dream consisted. I already knew about the conflicts of the patient. The dream contributed practically nothing novel in that respect. What it did was to enable me to estimate the severity of the conflict and judge just what effect it was having on the patient. In this case the special value of the dream was that it showed the dreamer was tending towards a special solution of his conflict, and since, in this case, the solution was suicide, with all the vastly important consequences which this solution would bring, the value of the dream was obvious. But, though less striking, the dream always has this value in helping the exact estimation of the personality of the dreamer and of the forces internal and external which are acting upon him. Thus, the two dreams of my patient with what I call the anti-quartermaster sentiment arose out of quite subsidiary and temporary conflicts, and had little immediate or direct importance in his treatment, but, nevertheless, they were of distinct value in enabling me to estimate the character of the dreamer. They enabled me to estimate the patient's mode of reaction towards the minor worries of life, and his perhaps overstrong sense of responsibility in his dealings with his fellow-men. They definitely assisted an exact diagnosis of his personality. A deeper analysis might have shown that the quartermaster was a surrogate for some other person, perhaps his father, and knowledge of this kind might possibly have helped the patient to readjust his life. If he had broken down as the result of the ordinary strains of civil life, some such deeper analysis would perhaps have been desirable. I mention this case here only to illustrate how even dreams dealing with minor temporary conflicts have their value in that estimation of personality which helps towards the successful treatment of psycho-neurosis.

The point I am trying to make now is that even when the physician is already well acquainted with a patient and his conflicts a dream may have a definite value in helping him to weigh the relative importance of different elements of a conflict, and to estimate more exactly the nature of the personality by which the conflict has to be solved. One value of the kind of analysis which I have been considering in this book is that it enables the more exact estimation of the finer shades in the diagnosis of the situation with which it is thè business of patient and physician to deal.

In this book, dealing primarily with the scientific aspect of a problem, or set of problems, I have so far only recorded dreams where an extensive knowledge of the dreamer has allowed me to utilise his dreams as evidence. I propose now to give a few examples of dreams related by patients of whom I knew comparatively little, in order to illustrate their value in diagnosis of a cruder kind.

I will begin with a dream related by a young pilot in the R.A.F. He had flown and fought for many months in France, and as the result of the strain was suffering from a mild anxiety state with unpleasant dreams which could, however, hardly be called nightmares, and were certainly not battle-dreams of the ordinary kind. Apparently there was not much wrong with him, and as was customary with my patients in the Air Force, I was only trying to make sure that he was not the subject of any special conflict, or, if he was, that he was dealing with it in the right way before sending him away for a holiday as a preliminary to return to duty. I failed to detect the existence of any youth conflict. He seemed the usual, cheerful, irresponsible kind of youth with whom one was accustomed to deal in the Air Force, very different from the man weighed down by responsibilities and anxieties with whom I had been accustomed to deal in the army. Though the generally unpleasant nature of his dreams made me suspect the existence of some conflict, none could be discovered. One morning, however, he related the following dream :

He was in gaol. He did not know and could not find out what offence he had committed, but he was sure of his innocence.

On inquiry into the incidents of the previous day he related that he had received a letter in the evening from a favourite uncle who was in prison as a conscientious objector. He was especially fond of this uncle, who had had much influence with him, and early in the war the patient had tended to sympathise with his uncle's views, so that there had been at one time a certain amount of conflict about enlisting. After joining, any doubts about the justifiability of war had completely disappeared, and, as I have already said, he had had a successful career as a pilot. As a result of the strain of active service, however, his doubts had reappeared. We had a conversation about the situation which hitherto he had not really attempted to face. Three days later his dreams had become much less disturbing, and a week later he was not only very much better in every respect, but he was having no dreams at all.

The dream I have described certainly put me on the traces of a conflict which was apparently so slight that the patient did not himself attach much importance to it. It is very improbable that he would have told me about it if I had not been put on its track by a dream. (I may mention that two days after the first dream he had another dream, from which he awoke feeling natural and comfortable, which appeared to depend on another minor conflict concerning uniform. In this dream he saw a balloon which came down, and a dozen strange-looking men got out of it. He went up to them and asked them by what authority they were in civilian clothes. Instead of answering they disappeared, and then he noticed that he was wearing an old tunic which did not belong to him.)

The dreamer was very young and looked even more youthful than his years. On the previous day he had been out in a new uniform and had noticed people looking at him. He had supposed that they were thinking that he had only just got his commission. In the dream he exerted authority and was wearing an old tunic.

In this case a dream led me to a conflict which I should probably otherwise have missed, chiefly because it seemed to the patient too trivial to be worth mention. In another case the conflict was more serious, and probably I should have discovered it sooner or later without a dream being needed. The patient held a commission in the Air Force, and had had severe concussion in a crash under painful circumstances in that his companion was killed. He was suffering from severe nightmares, from which he awoke sweating and frightened, of falling over cliffs and burning in his aeroplane, which is, of course, the chief dread of nearly every flying man. He was repressing vigorously and could not stand being in the dark, because the thoughts of flying repressed during the day then came into his mind. As usual in such a case my treatment was directed to enable him to deal with his crash and its consequences, as with any other experience of life. Owing to his leaving the hospital, I did not see him for some time, and when we met next he told me of a very painful dream, which had recurred on three successive nights. In this dream he was " carting about " a dead body wherever he went. He had a horror of the body and a dreadful feeling of anxiety because it was always with him. The dream ended by his going home and putting the dead body under his bed. The body was always in the same attitude, with hands over the shoulders, so that the palms were exposed. The body was that of a very big man with thick wrists and a greenish skin.

The patient had been in the army before he joined the R.F.C., and after some thought he remembered a day in 1916 when he had tried to jump a trench, and failing to clear it had unearthed a partially buried German, exposing the whole body. The hands of the corpse were in just the attitude of the dream, and there was also agreement in its general appearance. The chief feature of the manifest dream was thus accounted for. It remained to discover the deeper meaning, which was soon clear. Four days earlier he had discovered, after suspecting for some time, that he had acquired syphilis. He had much knowledge of this disease and was acquainted with the relation between it and general paralysis. At the same time he was engaged to be married. His immediate conflict was concerned with his relation to his fiancée, as he believed that there would be a danger of his incurring general paralysis as long as he lived. We discussed the matter fully. I naturally laid much stress on the necessity for thorough treatment and minimised the danger of any lifelong influence if this was undertaken.

On the following night he did not dream, and though the dream had previously recurred three nights running, he never had it again.

I have cited this dream for its practical value, but I cannot resist relating an element of the analysis of scientific interest. I was anxious to discover why the body of a dead German only seen momentarily two years earlier should have acted as the symbol of the syphilis with which he believed he was to be encumbered for the rest of his life. At first he could think of nothing which would connect this sight with any element of his conflict, until at last it occurred to him that just about the time he unearthed the German he had heard that the girl who had later become his fiancée, whom he had known for many years from childhood, had become engaged to someone else. He was very much upset and had become thoroughly reckless, but matters had gone better later, for she had broken her engagement and had become engaged to him. There was thus a definite association between his fiancée and the experience with the German with upturned palms.

THE DREAMS OF CHILDREN AND ANTARCTIC EXPLORERS

So far, I have been considering dreams to be attempted solutions of conflicts ; but now I must refer to certain types that appear at first sight to be obvious cases of wish-fulfilment, into which the element of conflict either does not seem to enter at all, or at any rate to be an obtrusive feature. One of these cases is that of the simple dreams of children, in which they attain in their dreams desires formed during the day. Having had no experience in the investigation of the dreams of children, it would be of little value to deal with this matter at length ; but I may note that the records of such dreams * show that the desires attained in them are often those, the satisfaction of which has been forbidden by parents or others during the day, where there are obvious grounds for the presence of a conflict. The same is probably true of the simple dreams of adults, which seem to be simple wish-fulfilments. Thus, the frequent dreams of soldiers in France that they were on leave were probably something more than the result of the natural and obvious

---

* See, for example, those recorded by Dr Kimmins in his book, *Children's Dreams.*

desire to be on leave. It is evident that in such cases there would be scope for conflicts arising out of the incompatibility between these desires and sentiments connected with military duty. One would like to know something about the character and general mental attitude of those who had dreams of this kind. A third type of dream which raises greater difficulty is that presented by the dreams experienced by members of Arctic and Antarctic Expeditions, especially dreams in which they enjoyed the pleasures of the table. Dreams of this kind have been recorded by Otto Nordenskjöld. Thus he writes : *

" Very illustrative of the direction of our innermost thoughts were our dreams, which were never more vivid and numerous than now. Even those of us who otherwise dreamed but seldom, had long stories to tell in the morning when we compared our latest experiences from this world of fantasy. All of our visions concerned the outer world, which now lay so distant from us, but were usually applied to our present circumstances. One of the most characteristic dreams was that where one of us fancied he had gone back to his school-bench in order to learn how to flay minia-ture seals, which were of a size just suitable for use in instructing a class. But meat and drink were usually the centres round which our dreams revolved. One of us who made a speciality of going to banquets in his visions was highly pleased one morning when he could relate that ' last night I managed to get through three courses.' Naturally, we were also busied in our visions with more impossible things, but the want of fantasy in almost all the dreams I had, or those which I heard related, was most apparent ; still, I think it would have been of great psychological interest had all these dreams been taken down."

* *Antarctica*, Otto Nordenskjöld and Gunnar Andersson, London, 1905, page 290.

Similar dreams have been frequent among the members of recent British Antarctic Expeditions, and I am indebted to Mr R. E. Priestley of Christ's College for much valuable information about them.

In his experience dreams of this kind fell into two classes, those in which the dreams were satisfied by a dream-meal, and those in which food only formed the subject-matter of the dreams. The meals enjoyed or only contemplated would vary from a mere snack to a twelve-course City dinner.

It is natural to regard dreams of this kind as simple wish-fulfilments. It seems natural that men whose dietary was confined to limited amounts of monotonous fare should have strong desires for food of a different kind, and that the dreams were simply the fulfilment of these desires. Mr Priestley tells me, however, that the desire for food was far from being always satisfied in these dreams. Several members of his party had dreams in which they imagined that there was a shop behind the hut in which they were living, which they had only to visit in order to obtain ample supplies of food. The dreamer would make his way out of the hut by the same laborious means as those necessary in real life, only to find on reaching the shop that it was early closing day. If the dreams were determined by wishes for food, these wishes were thus by no means always satisfied in sleep.

Another fact cited by Mr Priestley is very important in relation to the thesis which I am putting forward in this book. Mr Priestley tells me that in his opinion nothing was more the subject of conflicts during these expeditions than food. Dreams of the kind we are considering were especially frequent and definite when he was with a party whose food had to be very severely rationed. There were frequent occasions for conflict in connection with food, such as those arising out of finding a fragment of biscuit which had fallen during the process of distribution, or the opportunities presenting themselves while cooking. His evidence shows that during waking life there were present just those conflicts connected with food which on the hypothesis put forward in this book would have made food the natural subject of a conflict in sleep.

In all three of the special kinds of dream, which seem at first sight to furnish difficulties for the view that dreams depend on the activity of conflicts in sleep, it has been found that there are present the conditions necessary for conflict. It is a question, however, whether all wishes do not imply some degree of conflict. . There would be no occasion for a wish if there were not an obstacle of some kind to the attainment of the end to which the wish is directed. It is possible to speak of a dream as determined either by a wish or a conflict, and my objection to Freud is not so much to his expression of the purpose of a dream in terms of desire as to his view that dreams are necessarily the fulfilment of desire. I have not only tried to show that in many dreams wishes are not fulfilled but frustrated, and that in such cases the fate of the desire has a most important bearing on the nature of the affective aspect of the dream. The formula I propose has not only been made wider than that of Freud, in order to include every kind of dream, but, still more important, because it enables us to explain certain features of the affective aspect of dreams before which Freud's simpler formula is quite inadequate, if not indeed wholly helpless.

I may take this opportunity of giving an account of a dream related to me by Mr Priestley which admirably illustrates the main thesis of this book. Among the members of the Scott Expedition there was a Norwegian who was naturally divided in his wishes concerning the race to the South Pole by his having the same nationality as Amundsen, their rival. This Norwegian had a dream in which he was in the streets of Christiania when a telegram was put into his hands. On opening it he found a message, signed by Amundsen, saying that he had reached the Pole. We have here an almost perfect example of a dream as a solution of a conflict in accordance with the deeper wishes of the dreamer. During the day the Norwegian was an apparently whole-hearted adherent of the Expedition to which he belonged, and apparently really desired the success of his adopted country in the struggle upon which they were engaged, but in his sleep the youthful attitude reasserted itself, so that not only did his native country form the setting of the dream, but his countryman was the victor in the contest.

CHAPTER X

THE " PACIFIST " DREAM

THIS dream consists of two parts : an earlier, of which my recollection on waking was vague, though not perhaps more vague than my usual memory of dreams ; and a later part which I recollected with unusual definiteness.

Part I. I arrived at a place near the sea by train, and went to the house of a married friend, who seemed to be the composite image of two people, one of whom was a professor of physiology and the other a professor of another science. I will call the physiologist V and the other W. When I was packing up to go away, I put two numbers of a journal with a yellow cover in my Gladstone bag. I had the impression that these were numbers of the Austrian anthropological publication *Anthropos*. On the journey I had left things in the train, and on seeking them found a hard bowler hat and an umbrella in the rack of a railway carriage. I left the house for the train to go away, driving with my host and hostess. At a turning into a street I got out of the carriage in which we were driving. I do not know how I was dressed in this part of the dream.

Part II. I was in the house with the same friends, and went out of their front door into a large court-yard. I was told by my host to turn to the left, but instead of doing so I turned to the right. I did not find the door I expected. I was turning away when my host, whose personality had in this phase of the dream

165

changed in nature so as to resemble V more than W, called to me that I had gone the wrong way and must go to the left. I went to the left and found a small door in a corner of the courtyard on which was written " Physiologisches Practicum." I entered and went up a flight of stairs, at the top of which I was met by a man whom I could not identify with anyone I knew or had known. He was bandaged and had one arm in a sling. He greeted me and asked me if I was in practice. I said that I was working temporarily in the army, whereupon he asked after Professor Z, another English physiologist, and spoke about the work he had been doing. Though the man spoke English he was definitely thought of in the dream as a German professor. He was in civilian dress, while I had the impression that I was in uniform, though on waking I could not recall an image of myself in this dress.

On thinking over the dream, I recalled a number of events of the previous day which would have helped to determine the manifest content. I had lunched with Mrs A, with whom I had travelled to Australia just before the outbreak of the war. During lunch she had reminded me of a pamphlet with a yellow cover which had been lost on the voyage. This pamphlet was on an anthropological subject, and I also had two numbers of *Anthropos* with me on the voyage. This journal also has a yellow cover. We had talked about Professor and Mrs W, who had been fellow-travellers.

Professor V has a German name and lives at a place which had been mentioned in the course of a conversation during the evening preceding the dream.

One of my patients, whom I will call B, had been a fellow-guest at lunch. He had been to see me during the evening preceding the dream, and among other subjects we had talked about Germany, and I had told him of some of my experiences in that country as a student, when my interests had been largely physiological. The combination of dwelling-house and laboratory, which is unusual in England, frequently occurs in Germany, and I had been especially familiar with the combination in Heidelberg, where I had been the guest of Professor Kühne. Heidelberg was one of the places especially mentioned during the conversation in the evening.

During the day I had received a letter from Dr C, of New York, an American physician with a German name, of whom I had not previously heard. He had written to me about a paper I had published, entitled " Freud's Psychology of the Unconscious." The striking feature of my correspondent's letter was his pleasure, tinged with wonder, at what he called my courage in venturing to deal with a topic which was at the time the object of so much contempt and obloquy in England. I remembered that the German name of my correspondent had led me to consider whether his pleasure was only due to the general character of my article, or whether he might have been influenced by its final words, which mentioned the Austrian nationality of Freud. These words had reference to the fact that several recent writers in the English medical press had regarded Freud's nationality as good evidence for the worthlessness of his views.

I have here put together facts which serve to explain various features of the manifest content, but long before this survey was concluded I had found my thoughts led to matters which pointed to the existence of a definite mental conflict. B, the patient who had been my fellow-guest at lunch, with whom I had had the conversation in the evening, was not suffering from any form of psycho-neurosis, but was in the hospital on account of his adoption of a pacifist attitude while on leave from active service. During the afternoon I had finished reading *Under Fire*, the translation of Barbusse's *Sur le Feu*, and during the evening I had looked through the *English Review* for the month, which dealt with problems of peace and war, and had put the magazine down in the middle of an article by Gorki. My general reading at this time was leading me towards a belief that the economic position of Germany was creating a situation which made peace by negotiation possible, and one article in the *English Review* had put this point of view in so striking a way that I had found myself in a frame of mind more favourable to peace by negotiation than I had ever known before. I had read this journal, as well as Barbusse's book, on the recommendation of B, partly in order to help me to understand his position. During the analysis I remembered quite clearly that when I was reading the *Review* I had thought of the situation that would arise if my task of converting a patient from his " pacifist errors " to the conventional attitude should have as its result my own conversion to his point of view. My attitude throughout the war had been clearly in favour of fighting until Germany recognised defeat, and though the humorous side of the imagined situation struck me more than its serious aspect, there can be little doubt that there was a good opening for conflict and repression. Though my manifest attitude was definitely in favour of war to the finish, I had no doubt about the existence of a very keen desire that the war should end as soon as possible for the egoistic motive that I might get back to my proper studies, which had been interrupted by the war. I have no doubt that this egoistic motive was always active beneath the surface. I was aware that if I had been acting solely in my own immediate interests I should have wished the war to come to an end at once, regardless of future consequences. There were thus the grounds for a definite conflict in my mind between a " pacifist " tendency dictated by my own interests on the one hand, and, on the other, opinions based partly on reasoned motives, partly on conventional adherence to the views of the majority, in favour of a fight to the finish. The article in the *English Review* may be assumed to have reinforced the egoistic side of the conflict by providing the rational support that, owing to the supposed economic ruin of Germany, peace by negotiation had become possible. The conversation with B must also have served to stimulate the conflict, though it is not easy to say which side of the conflict would have been strengthened.

The general character of the dream being thus referable to a conflict arising out of my attitude towards the war, it remained to discover how the various features of the manifest imagery of the dream formed an appropriate expression of the conflict. In the first part of the dream the incident which stood out most clearly in my memory was the search for certain lost articles and the finding of a hat and umbrella in the rack of a railway carriage. These two articles may be regarded as symbols of the civilian, the umbrella particularly being an article which is absolutely tabooed while in uniform. Finding them in the dream may be regarded as a symbol of the return to civilian dress and habits which the end of the war would bring.

The chief feature of the second dream was that, though it was not explicitly recognised while I was dreaming, I was evidently visiting a German laboratory, and the inscription on the door makes it clear that it was a physiological laboratory. My reception in the laboratory was of just such a kind as I had frequently experienced on visits to Germany about twenty years before, when, as I have already mentioned, my interests were largely physiological. The dream thus reproduced a state of affairs which formed an appropriate representation of peace with Germany. The incidents of this part of the dream not only implied peace, but also the restoration of the friendly relations between the scientific men of the two countries which existed before the war and was still more definite in the student days twenty years ago, which the dream reproduced.

The appearance of the journal *Anthropos* in the first part of the dream was significant, for though edited and published in Austria, it has an international character, and publishes its articles in French, Italian and English, as well as in the German language. This journal thus forms a fitting symbol of international peaceful relations.

A feature of the dream, which stood out very clearly in my recollection afterwards, was that I was directed by my host to turn to the left, but went instead to the right, and only found the laboratory when I was recalled and obeyed the original directions. It seems highly significant that Professor V, who now definitely dominated in the composite personality of my host, was a physiologist with a German name and ancestry, who would thus fittingly symbolise the reconciliation of the two nations in science.* It may be noted that before the war I had a firm belief in the value of scientific co-operation as a step towards international friendship, and that the war had given a rude shock to this belief. The dream thus revived an attitude which had been strong before the war.

Still more significant was my change of direction in the dream. If my going to the left, as directed by my host, had symbolised my movement in the pacifist direction, it would have been a movement contrary to all my opinions since the outbreak of the war, which had been definitely of the " fight to a finish " kind. The incidents of the dream thus symbolised a move-

* I have some reason to believe that Professor W, the other element of the composite host of the dream, would be a fitting symbol of the "fight to the finish" attitude.

170

ment, directed from without, in the pacifist direction, to which I failed to respond at first in the dream, and only obeyed after the application of a second stimulus from the dream-personage who symbolised the resumption of friendly relations with Germany.

One image of the dream which remains to be considered is that the German professor was bandaged and had his arm in a sling. I suggest that this was a symbol of a belief that Germany had been severely damaged by the war, so much so as to be no longer dangerous to the world. The idea that Germany was ruined economically had been prominent in my mind during the evening preceding the dream as the chief condition which made peace by negotiation possible.

Another feature of the dream which may be significant is that during the analysis I was uncertain whether I had been in uniform, although I was sure that the German professor was in civilian dress. The interest of my being in uniform or not was that it had a definite connection with the conflict which I suppose to underlie the dream, and especially with my relation to the patient B. So long as I was an officer of the R.A.M.C., and of this my uniform was the obvious symbol, my discussions with B on his attitude towards the war were prejudiced by my sense that I was not a free agent in discussing the matter, but that there was the danger that my attitude might be influenced by my official position. As a scientific student whose only object should be the attainment of what I supposed to be truth, it was definitely unpleasant to me to suspect that the opinions which I was uttering might be influenced by the needs of my position, and I was fully aware of an element of constraint in my relations with B on this account. So long as I was in uniform I was not a free agent, and though no one can be a free agent during a war, it was a definite element in my situation at the time that my official position might be influencing the genuineness of the views I was expressing in my conversations with B. On the other hand, there was the much cruder satisfaction at being in uniform during the war which, in common with most people, though in general below the surface, I detected in myself at times. It is perhaps significant in relation to this conflict that, though the question whether I was in uniform or not was definitely present in the thoughts immediately following the dream, it was not a question which I was able to answer.

Not only does this dream as a whole thus serve to express a complex conflict which was going on in my mind at the time, but there is not a single important element of the manifest dream which fails to form a suitable symbol of some element of the conflict. Especially prominent were the symbols of the wish for the restoration of peace, which I suppose to be the most powerful motive in the conflict. There is no question that the egoistic drive was in favour of peace, and that the effect of the article which I had read during the evening preceding the dream had been to reinforce this egoistic impulse by motives of a rational kind in the direction that existing conditions, and especially the battered economic state of Germany, now made a peace by negotiation possible.

One interest of the dream I have just interpreted is that it had a number of features which illustrate its regressive character, and in this case it is possible to date the regression more or less accurately to about twenty years earlier. The hat which I found in the first part of the dream was of the kind known as a bowler, which I had not worn for at least fifteen, probably twenty, years. I can date the regular use of a Gladstone bag exactly to twenty years earlier (1897). My visits to the laboratory in Heidelberg, which were clearly recalled during the analysis, took place in 1896. I am therefore able in this case to assign several of the symbols utilised in the dream to a definite period about twenty years before the occurrence of the dream. Moreover, though Professor V was still alive, and I had seen him not long before, he occupied a much more important place in my life twenty years ago than at the time of the dream. Most of the symbolism of the dream thus belonged to young adult age, when my aspirations after the international scientific relations, which found expression in the dream, were especially strong. If my position be accepted that the dream is an attempted solution of a conflict in accordance with the attitude proper to the level of mental development which is active at the existing depth of sleep, the dream was expressing, by means of the imagery and modes of thought of twenty years, a desire for peace which formed one side of the conflict to which the dream was due. An egoistic wish that the war should end had been strongly reinforced during the evening preceding the dream by motives of a rational kind. Thoughts of renewed scientific relations of an international kind had found expression in the dream by means of imagery from a period of life when interest in such international relations had been especially strong. The young adult whose personality was finding expression in this dream underwent in it experiences which meant the fulfilment, not only of the manifest desires of this time of life, but also the deeper craving for peace of the older man whose personality was the actual subject of the conflict.

The special interest of this dream is that the whole experience has a striking unity. Every feature of its manifest content can be brought into definite relation with the conflict which I suppose to underlie the dream. Most of the incidents of the dream are definitely connected with the friendly relations between the scientific men of Germany and Great Britain which would again become possible with the peace, the desire for which was the essential leading motive. The dream has, in addition, several minor points of interest.

In the first place, I may mention that though I have recorded the dream as one, it consisted definitely of two parts, and might possibly be regarded as two distinct dreams, the first of which was recollected indistinctly on account of its earlier occurrence. If this view be taken, we should have another example of the reference of two dreams occurring in one night to a common content. A second feature of interest is that the dream affords a very good example of a composite personality. As I have mentioned, there is some reason to believe that the two persons who formed the composite image represented different sides in the conflict upon which the dream depended, and it is of especial interest that the element in the compound, which certainly represented the international as opposed to the national side of the conflict, should have become more evident at the phase of the dream when the international aspect was being so clearly satisfied, and that he should have taken so important a part in the proceedings which led to this satisfaction.

Another point of interest is that this dream affords an example of the occurrence of right and left, to which so great a significance is attached by psycho-analysts. It is noteworthy here that the direction which symbolised a movement towards peace and international relations should be towards the left, while right was the direction which was taken when the dreamer disobeyed instructions and turned away from that part of the courtyard which contained the building which, according to the general character of the dream, would seem to symbolise the strongest desire. If we are to follow the psycho-analytic school in their belief that right always symbolises good and left bad, we have to suppose that to the dream-personality peace and international relations were regarded as bad. It seems far more likely that in this case " right " and " left " had reference to the customary means of denoting Conservative and Liberal tendencies, especially on the Continent. I was especially familiar at the time with the use of these expressions in the extracts from foreign journals published in the *Cambridge Magazine*, which I read regularly, and a movement to the left in such journals is a regular symbolic expression for Liberal tendencies. There can be no question that the movement towards international relations is especially characteristic of the Liberal parties of the world, and hostility to such aims occurs in association with Conservatism. If this explanation does not appeal to the psycho-analytic school, I can only suggest that the situation with which the dream-personality was dealing in this dream was too complicated to be viewed from the " *simpliste* " ethical standpoint from which they are accustomed to regard the dream.

SYMBOLISM

A striking feature of the dream which I have considered is its exemplification of use of symbols. The return to civilian life was represented by a hat and umbrella ; the return to international friendship by a journal which publishes papers in four languages, and also by an English scientist with German name and ancestry ; Germany in a state of peace but severely damaged through the war by a German professor bandaged and with his arm in a sling. Moreover, these symbolic expressions are of exactly the same kind as others recorded in this book. They are of the same kind as the representation of a person in an incongruous situation by a cup and saucer, an object in a game of billiards ; of rowing as a symbol of return to life in Cambridge; of an ichthyosaurus as a symbol of a rapacious quartermaster.

At the same time the interpretation of these objects as symbolic differs very greatly from that which would be given by the psycho-analytic school, and I propose to conclude with a brief consideration of this difference.

Both Freud and Jung with their respective schools are coming to agree closely in their acceptance of certain symbols as common to mankind, by means of which it is often possible to interpret dreams without the necessity of resorting to free association or other methods of analysis. According to Freud, the hat and such long articles as an umbrella are universal symbols of the male genital organ, and I am perfectly aware that my search for these articles in the " pacifist " dream will be interpreted by many of my readers on lines very different from those which I have myself followed. Similarly, there will doubtless be many who will interpret the snake in the two dreams of my suicidal patient on the lines that the snake is a universal phallic symbol, and will explain the dreams in a way very different from that which I have adopted.

In considering this subject I will begin by saying that I am prepared to go far towards accepting the view that there is an extensive agreement in the use of certain objects as symbols of certain other objects. Thus, there are obvious reasons why the male genital organ should be represented by a long object and the female genital organ by one of a rounder form, and I am also prepared to agree with Freud in the view that sexual objects and processes are especially likely to be represented in the dream symbolically rather than directly. I am therefore quite prepared to find a widespread tendency to symbolise the male sexual organ in dreams by long objects and the female organ by round objects. It is a long step from this, however, to the universalisation of this use of symbols which is discernible in Freud's recent work and has become definite among his disciples, here, as usual, far less critical than their master. Here, again, as usual, we are asked by the psycho-analysts to accept this universal symbolism merely on their word and with very little evidence. One of my reasons for publishing my own dreams is to provide evidence, which seems to me of some degree of cogency, that the symbols to which a universal sexual significance is attached, may at least in some cases bear a meaning of a different kind.

Evidence derived from the dreams of some of my patients has led me to believe that in many cases the symbols to which a universal sexual significance is attached by Freud often have this meaning, and I propose now to accept this position and inquire into its meaning. Accepting provisionally the view that the snake is frequently the symbol of the male sexual organ, let us inquire how this association between the two objects has come about. Freud seems definitely inclined to regard the association as innate, and that it is a universal among mankind, because we inherit it from our ancestors. In other words, according to Freud, the association is to be classed with the instincts and other forms of inherited capacity. Such a view implies an extraordinary neglect of the mental complexity of childhood, a neglect which is the more extraordinary in those who have done so much to reveal this complexity. There is no question that the mind of a child is extraordinarily receptive and that it absorbs vast amounts of unsuspected knowledge. We need far more exact observations about the nature of the childish environment of those whose dream-symbolism is studied before we can accept either the universal or the instinctive character of any form of this symbolism. To Jung and to the disciples of Jung this universality of symbolisms is even more important than to Freudians, for it is upon this belief that there is founded the concept of the collective unconscious which plays so great a part in their system.

Both Freud and Jung and their disciples are now accustomed to support their views concerning innate symbols by evidence derived from the comparative study of belief and custom, but their examples are chiefly drawn from Indo-European culture where we know of the existence of a common tradition. The possibility cannot be excluded that this common tradition reaches the individual in infancy, childhood and youth through the intermediation of parents, nurses, school-fellows, the overhearing of chance conversations, and many other sources. If, however, symbolism of the universal kind exists, it should be universal among mankind, and of this Freud and Jung and their disciples have as yet given no evidence. Indeed, such work as they have published on this subject has been fragmentary and uncritical. I once asked one of the leading disciples of Jung in this country for an example of some universal belief which could be taken as an example of Jung's primordial thought-image and he chose the representation of good by right and of evil by left. He was wholly ignorant of the fact that there is no evidence whatever of the association among most peoples of the earth, and that a vast number of their languages are wholly devoid of words for right and left, orientation which we perform by means of these concepts being effected by means of the direction of prevailing winds or other crude methods of a kind similar to our orientation by means of the points of the compass. Even so near at home as Scotland the concepts of right and left are so vague, or have so little interest, that it was not long ago customary to orientate by means of points of the compass. A person was not said to part his hair on the right or left, but to the east or west.

SYMBOLISM IN DREAMS

If I had myself to answer the question I put to the disciple of Jung, I could have chosen better instances. There are many facts of ritual and belief which point to the very wide distribution of certain forms of symbolism, but it is a question whether this wide distribution is not directly due to a far more extensive spread of the traditions present in Indo-European culture than is generally supposed. Certainly, there are many features of distribution which point to such diffusion. Thus, in Melanesia, many of the symbols which have a wide distribution are not common to the whole community, but form part of a secret ritual, known only to specially initiated persons, and not common to the general body of the community. I have shown reason to believe * that these secret rituals are those of bodies of immigrants from elsewhere who were led by certain motives to practise their religious or magical rites in secret. The nature of their symbols are no more evidence of universal thought-images than a piece of information given by me here, taken by one of you to Australia or America and there handed on, is evidence that the idea thus conveyed is innate and has welled up from the collective unconscious of the Australian or American. To such an argument the disciple of Jung may reply that even if it can be proved that the use of a symbol has been transmitted from one place to another, say from Egypt to Melanesia, we have still to explain why it should have taken root in its new home and become part of the mental endowment of the people to whom it was transmitted. They will argue that there must have been something in the mental structure of the people to whom it was transmitted which led to this acceptance, and the disciples of Jung will say that this acceptance was due to its compatibility with the content of the collective unconscious. There might be something to be said

* *History of Melanesian Society,* 1914.

in favour of this point of view, and perhaps there would be much to say for it if the transmitted belief were universally accepted by whole populations : but when we find such transmitted beliefs confined to the few, and only imparted to individuals, perhaps at relatively advanced periods of their lives, the need for innate ideas compatible with those which have been introduced becomes less strong. We need far more evidence concerning the nature of the transmitted symbols, before there can be established even a probable case for innate symbolism or for such a state as the collective unconscious of Jung.

APPENDIX 1

In the Freudian scheme of the psychology of the dream the main biological function of the dream is to protect the sleeper from being awakened either by external stimuli to his senses, or by the internal stimuli provided by unpleasant thoughts or emotions. In the case of unpleasant stimuli to the sense-organs it is supposed that it is the function of the dream to transform the sensations which these stimuli would occasion in the waking life into images devoid of such tendency to awake. On the other hand, it is supposed that unpleasant thoughts and affects are similarly transformed, and thus deprived of that character which would lead the sleeper to awake. The dream is regarded as the guardian of sleep and not its disturber. It is believed to act as a kind of safety-valve to the unconscious.*

As I have pointed out elsewhere,† there is much reason to believe that in many of the forms assumed by the dream in man, it has come to have this function, but there are certain features of the dream, and certain forms of dream, which can hardly be reconciled with this view of the biological function of the dream. Especially is this the case with the nightmare The occurrence of this form of dream in the young, and as part of the regression of psycho-neurosis, makes it probable that this is the primitive form of the dream,

* *Die Traumdeutung,* 5te Auflage, Leipzig and Wien, 1919, pages 163 and 429.
† *Dreams and Primitive Culture,* Manchester, 1917.

and that the pleasant or indifferent dream of the healthy adult is a modification of this primitive form of the psychologising process.

If now we turn our attention to the nightmare or similar form of dream, which has a more or less sudden awakening as one of its most definite characters, we find that a pronounced feature is exaggeration of affect. The nightmare shows a degree of affect altogether out of proportion to the external or internal stimulus by which the dream has been set up. Is it possible to discover any biological conditions which would have made this exaggeration of affect serviceable to the animal ?

In considering this problem let us deal first with the isolated individual. It is evident that with the biological function of sleep as the means of physiological recuperation, there must have been associated a considerable degree of danger. For hours at a time and at a period of the day when his enemies may be especially active, an animal is accustomed to pass into a state of passivity and immobility which must seriously prejudice the success of its normal reactions to danger. As I have pointed out elsewhere,* there is reason to believe that with this passivity and immobility there goes a considerable degree of sensibility to the stimuli to which it would react in the waking state. There is even some reason to believe that there may be some heightening of the sensibility which is present in the waking state, but even if there be such heightening, the animal would be seriously prejudiced by the loss of time occupied in the process of awakening, by the business of adapting the limbs and other parts of the body to the appropriate mode of action and by putting the process of reaction into practice. It is evident that the reaction of the animal to danger would be greatly assisted if there were present in

* *Instinct and the Unconscious.*

sleep some kind of mechanism by which the animal began to adapt its behaviour to danger while still asleep. If this mechanism also helped to awaken, it would still further increase its helpfulness to the sleeping animal. I suggest that the dream has such functions. That, whatever may be the function of the dream in man, its function in the lower animals is to awaken in the presence of danger and to set in action, even while the animal is still asleep, the process by which it will be enabled to meet the danger in the appropriate manner. Thus, if the appropriate reaction is that of aggression, with its accompanying affect of anger, it would be highly serviceable if the affect of anger arose with its appropriate bodily setting in sleep and thus adapted the animal, even while still asleep, to those aggressive movements which it would normally adopt as soon as possible after waking. If, on the other hand, the reaction appropriate to the animal were flight, with its affective accompaniment of fear, the dream would take that form of fear which would normally be associated with the disposition of the body to the movements adapted to remove the animal as speedily as possible from the source of danger.

If now we pass from the individual animal to the herd, we find a motive not only for the presence of affect in the dream, but also for its presence in an exaggerated form, a form for which there is no adequate motive in the case of the individual creature. If the member of the herd which reacts most speedily to the sensory indications of danger does not merely react, but begins before waking to utter cries or growls, or to give other indications of danger, its behaviour will awaken the whole herd and serve to put it on its guard more speedily than if it had to wait till its most sensitive member had been itself awakened before it could give the warning signal. The association of animals in herds would provide a biological motive for the dream, even if no such motive could be found for its usefulness to the individual animal.

It is not possible to prove that the dreams of animals have this useful function. We know far too little of the behaviour of animals in sleep to provide evidence of any great value for or against the hypothesis I have put forward. The sleeping behaviour of the dog does not, however, contradict it. There is little doubt that the dog is an animal which normally reacts to danger by means of the instinct of aggression. However larger or more powerful an approaching dog may be, the first and immediate reaction is one of aggression with its characteristic growl, and it is only when this form of reaction has been shown to be wholly inappropriate that the animal resorts to the alternative reaction of flight. It is therefore of interest that when a dog suggests by its behaviour in sleep that it is dreaming, the reactions seem always to take the form of growls, similar to those by which it responds in the waking state to the presence of another of its species.

In the absence of evidence it would be little profit in speculating further on the biological function of dreams in animals, first as an agent to awaken the animal, and secondly to adapt it even while still sleeping to the behaviour it would normally adopt on waking. It will be of interest, however, to consider how this early function of dreams has been in man modified to so great an extent that it has been possible to regard the dream not as an instrument of awaking, but as a guardian of sleep.

In considering this subject it will be natural to begin with the nightmare, or other similar form of dream, the occurrence of which in childhood and psycho-neurosis has led me to regard it as the primitive form of the dream.

The difficulty with which we are here confronted is that in the nightmare there is an excess of affect, and of physiological reactions accompanying the affect, which would make the dream of little or no value if it were produced by an actual danger. The pallor, coldness, and sweating of a characteristic nightmare are such as would not only deprive the dreamer of all possibility of putting into action the movements by which the danger might be avoided, but it might even obstruct the reaction by flight. The whole reaction is of a kind associated with the unserviceable reaction by collapse to which mankind seems to be especially liable when his normal modes of reaction fail.

We are here brought up against the same problem as that with which we are faced when we consider the existence of collapse as one of man's modes of reaction to danger.* In the case of the dream, however, it is possible to suggest one way in which the excessive reaction of the nightmare may be explained. In the case of the animal considered in the earlier part of this chapter the reaction which occurs in sleep is that habitual to the animal. I have supposed that in the dream the animal is only experiencing an affect and exhibiting behaviour which are habitual to it in the waking state. In man, on the contrary, the affects and reactions present in the nightmare are not only not habitual, but they have in most persons been the objects of a life-long suppression, a suppression so successful that in a state of health the subject of the nightmare may have been repeatedly exposed to danger without experiencing even in a slight degree the reactions which show themselves in the nightmare. There is much reason, however, to believe that the excessive reactions of the nightmare of the adult are not due to the removal of this suppression, but are the result of a different though allied process of witting repression.

It is thus possible to bring the nightmare and other crude forms of human dream into relation with the

* *Instinct and the Unconscious.*

185

hypothesis that the primary function of the dream is to awaken an animal and adapt it to the appropriate form of reaction to danger. It remains to consider how the dream has been modified so as to present the highly varied forms and apparently very different functions which it seems to exhibit in the healthy adult human being.

I may remark at once that if the view here put forward is valid, there is an intimate relation between the dream and the instinct of self-preservation. According to this view the dream is primarily the means by which the animal is assisted to react successfully to danger even while asleep. Let us now turn to inquire whether there is any other way in which the dream might be useful to an animal, and let us begin with the parental instinct. Here we have not only the function of protecting the young from danger which would act in much the same way as the reaction to danger of the animal itself, especially in so far as the reaction by aggression is concerned, but we have to consider the needs of the young for food if the relation between parent and child is such that the young will only thrive if frequently supplied with food by the parent. In the case of mammals the function of the mother in connection with lactation would provide a possible motive for the dream. If in a suckling mother dreams of being suckled were aroused by the cries of her young, it would be possible for the young to obtain what they need without awaking the mother. A suitable dream would enable the suckling mother to adjust her movements to the needs of her young without waking. We have here a motive opposed to that which serves to produce the reaction to danger whereby the dream would act as the guardian of sleep exactly as it is supposed to act by Freud. At the same time it will be of the utmost importance that the mother shall react in a wholly different way if danger threatens her young and herself. In this case the dream would act as an awakener or as a guardian of sleep according to the nature of the stimulus by which the dream has been produced.

As I have shown elsewhere,* one of the characters of sleep is that it is a state in which the sleeper is not only able to react to sensory stimuli, but is capable of discriminating between those which call for activity and those of an indifferent kind. If an animal which had acquired the power of dreaming as a means of being awakened, and of being adapted to danger even while still asleep, were to dream and awaken at every sound or smell, the dream would soon lose its useful function, or would have such secondary effects in frequent disturbance of sleep as would more than counterbalance the useful function. It would be essential that the animal should at the same time acquire the power of discriminating between sensory stimuli indicative of danger and those which had no such significance. The power of sensory discrimination in sleep would be a necessary accompaniment of the dream if the serviceable nature of this process were not made useless by excess. When, therefore, the mammalian mother found the dream useful as a means of guarding sleep, there would already be present that power of discrimination between stimuli of different kinds which the double character of the dream would make necessary. Instead of leading to activity adapted to meet danger, stimuli of a certain kind would produce dreams which would help to maintain instead of disturbing sleep.

If now we turn from the parental instinct to that of sex, we find a still more definite motive for dreams of a protective kind. There is reason to believe that sensations of smell are especially powerful as stimuli to instinctive sexual reactions, and where animals con-

* *Instinct and the Unconscious.*

gregate together during sleep these stimuli would continue and would tend to awaken. If these stimuli acted in the manner customary in the waking life, sleep would be disturbed and a similar disturbance would also be produced by stimuli to the sexual organs produced by fleas or other parasites. Some kind of process by which stimuli of these kinds would be deprived of their awakening effect would be highly serviceable to the animal as guardians of sleep. I suggest that we have here the biological motive for the transformation of the dream, which is a feature of the most characteristic dreams of man. I suggest that as man developed from being something more than a creature dominated by his crude instincts, this transforming function of the dream was utilised in the interest of other factors which would tend to disturb his sleep, but that the original character of the dream as an awakening agent still persisted to show itself in childhood and in the pathological regressions of psycho-neurosis.

If it be one of the most frequent functions of the dream in man so to transform the results of sexual stimulation, external or internal, that they do not awake the sleeper, this would only be in direct continuity with a biological function which has been serviceable as a guardian of sleep in all those animals whose sexual activity is developed on the same lines as in man. Moreover, the need for such transformation would become especially great when the sexual function, in place of being limited to certain seasons, came, as has happened in man, to be more or less continuously active. If the transforming function of the dream came into existence as a means of protection against too frequent stimulation of the sexual instinct in sleep, it is natural that this instinct should serve as one of the most frequent, if not the most frequent of, occasions for the process of transformation.

APPENDIX II

THE comparison between dreams and myths in Chapter
IX is so brief that it is likely to give rise to miscon-
ception. Moreover, it cannot be regarded as a true
expression of the views of Dr Rivers. This is revealed
in his statements on symbolism in Chapter X of this
book and his Presidential Address to the Folk-lore
Society (*Folk-lore*, March 1922). Hence, I am sure
that if he had lived to prepare his manuscript for
publication he would not have allowed the following
passage in Chapter IX to appear in this form : " It
is probable that, at the stage of social development,
of which myth-formation is especially characteristic,
there is a similar identification, and that every natural
object to which man's attention is especially directed
is thought of as having human characteristics and is
endowed with such human characters as the power
of speech and the capacity for locomotion. That
animals should talk is just as natural to the man of
lowly culture as it is natural to the dream-consciousness
of the most highly civilised of mankind." But in
the particular dream used by Dr Rivers for the purpose
of this comparison, one of his patients personified
certain rivers and attributed to them human powers of
sympathy and speech simply because these streams
were identified with Dr Rivers himself, for the specific
reason that he happened to have the name " Rivers."

During the last seven years Dr Rivers repeatedly
discussed with me the late Sir Edward Tylor's concept
of animism, belief in which he had abandoned long ago ;

and during the last three years he had come more and more fully to accept the view, which Mr W. J. Perry and I have been urging, that there is no evidence to prove the personification of any natural object or to attribute to animals or plants human qualities or powers except when some specific factor, such as led the patient to personify " rivers " in his dream, came into play to cause confusion between the inanimate object (or animal or plant) and some human being.

In fact, the patient's dream about the personified " rivers " is an exact illustration of what ancient literature reveals concerning the origin of myths. Osiris was identified with the river Nile, or, in other words, his originally human qualities and powers were confused with the river's. In this way the river became personified. Osiris was the dead king who devised irrigation : the story of his beneficence as the controller of the life-giving water became transformed, after frequent repetition by story-tellers, into the belief that the dead king himself was the life-giver, and he became identified with the river, which bestowed the vitalising powers attributed to the dead king. This brought about not only the personification of the river, but also the apotheosis of the dead king, who became the god Osiris. The explanation of the process of personification of so many natural objects, and the attribution of human qualities to so many animals, is now known to be due to similarly arbitrary and specific causes that one is justified in doubting whether, in fact, " every natural object to which man's attention is specially directed is thought of," by relatively primitive people or by any people, " as endowed with such human characteristics as the power of speech and the capacity for locomotion." In my book *The Evolution of the Dragon* I have collected some evidence in opposition to this view. I refer to the matter here because I do not think Dr Rivers consciously intended to put forward a claim which does not really help his argument, but exposes it to destructive criticism such as he himself would have brought to bear upon it.

Dr Rivers has stated in this book that he " distrusts analogies." No experiment of this nature has proved more disastrous than the attempts of Freud, Jung, and their followers, to institute analogies between dreams and myths, for the sexual symbolism which plays so prominent a part in the former (though not in the way Freud and his followers assume) is altogether unimportant in myth. The fundamental motive underlying myth is the search for the elixir of life, prompted by the instinct of self-preservation, and not by the conflicts arising out of the desire to gratify the sexual instinct, as so often happen in dreams.

The phrase " the stage of social development of which myth-formation is especially characteristic " and the reference to composite animals are so out of harmony with the whole conception of this book that I feel sure Dr Rivers would have modified or completely deleted these passages, or made clear that he intended to convey ideas vastly different from the manifest content of the phraseology. It is misleading to speak of a myth-making phase in man's history, since myths have been developing ever since the first human beings acquired the power of speech. That certain myths survive while millions of others are merely ephemeral depends upon (1) the nature of the appeal particular stories make to man's instinct of self-preservation ; and (2) the restraining influence which the growth of knowledge and the definition of critical insight impose upon the development of phantasy.

I think Dr Rivers would have defined his ambiguous phrase to mean that there was a certain phase in man's social development when most of the really persistent myths of world-wide distribution arose. But this was not due to any mental idiosyncrasy or stage of psychical evolution. At a particular stage the growth of knowledge seemed to encourage the belief that a real elixir of life might be discovered, and the fame of this possibility made a universal appeal to man's deepest instinct, which was not restrained by a comprehension of natural phenomena. In later times myths continued to develop ; and the present age is certainly as prolific in such phantasies as any earlier period : but the fuller knowledge of natural phenomena and the critical insight that such knowledge gives tend to cut short the careers of most modern myths.

The problem of composite animals I have discussed elsewhere, and Dr Rivers accepted my views. Hence, I do not think he would have attached any real importance to the analogy he tentatively suggested (on page 148) between the composite creatures that figure in the dragon myth and the composite formations of dream-symbolism.

G. E. S.

INDEX

INDEX

INDEX

Lightning Source UK Ltd.
Milton Keynes UK
UKOW05f0128300713

214582UK00001B/26/P